Herb Brooks also wrote *Investing With A Computer: a Time-Series Analysis Approach,* TAB Books.

The Voter's Revenge

Herb Brooks

First edition

First printing. Aug. 1995

Illustrations by John T. Lewis
Cover by Laurel Brooks (color) and John T. Lewis (drawings)

ISBN 0-9647166-0-7
ISSN 1083-5407

Manufactured in the United States of America.
Voter's Revenge Press
Box 394
Youngtown, AZ 85363

Dedicated to the world's voters.

Acknowledgements. Dr. Donald M. Swingle, Jim Drake, Prof. James L. Payne, Dr. Werner Chilton, Prof. Richard Girard, Prof. Milan Zeleny, Basil Barwell, Prof. Howard Westing, and most of all my wife Elizabeth and my daughter Laurel. *None* of these people agree with everything I write, but they encouraged me to finish the project anyway.

CORRECTION

Corruption is a chameleon. When looters have abused "the system" beyond the tolerance of voters, the legislators apply "surface treatment": they paint the corruption a different color and call it by different names. PAC was a new name in the 1970s, but now its smell is out of the package, and less than half of the corrupt financing is labeled "PAC". Some of it is called "soft money", but it smells the same, and its name will be changed in time.

So in this section, substitute "self-serving campaign financing" for "PAC". The Center for Responsive Politics and Project Vote Smart (page 26) report all of it that they can find. I am indebted to Ellen Miller, Executive Director of the Center for this correction.

PREFACE

● In the 1970s our economy got sick (Chapter 1).

● The cause of that sickness was wasteful spending by Congress[1], motivated by PACs (Chapter 2).

The *bad* news is: Congress is not now to be trusted with one more dollar, or one more function like medical care.

The *good* news is: The problems with Congress will be easy for the *voters* to solve.

What Can Be Done?

What can you do to stop the waste? Write a letter to your congressman? Lots of luck. *Every* candidate promises reform, but most campaign promises are just hot air -- they didn't happen in 1992, or 1980, or 1976.

Vote for Republicans instead of Democrats? That didn't help in 1980, and it didn't help in 1994[2]. Only the words change; the spending and the waste still go on. Chapter 4 explains why.

Is it too late to do something about it?

NO!

But we have to do the right things.

Can *anything* positive be done? You bet! *We voters* can stop it. All we need to do is to stop voting bribe-takers into office.

To Stop The Waste, How should you vote?

• Vote for the candidate who has taken the least money from selfish PACs.

All the major-party front-runners for President have disqualified themselves by collecting millions, ***more than one year before*** the election. Maybe it's "third-party" time!

• Never vote for a candidate just because he brings home "pork"; it doesn't pay off (Chapter 2).

• When in doubt, vote against the incumbent; he is difficult to unseat, because he gets the most PAC money.

Or don't vote -- it dilutes the informed votes.

Chapter 5 has more voting suggestions.

We invented our form of democracy. Now it's time to *re*invent[3] it.

Notes:
1. "Congress" includes both houses: the Senate as well as the House of Representatives.
2. Goodgame, Dan (1995), "Here Comes the Pork: The Republicans who promised to make historic budget cuts are cutting some sweet deals as well", *Time,* July 17 p 18-21.
3. Gross, Martin L. (1993) *A Call for Revolution: How Washington is Strangling America -- and How to Stop it,* Ballantine Books.

CONTENTS

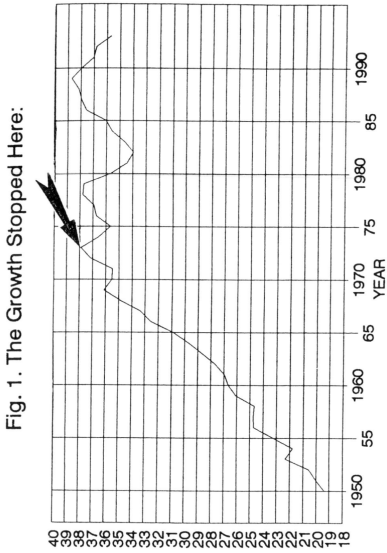

Fig. 1. The Growth Stopped Here:

Chapter 1
OUR ECONOMY IS SICK

Is your *real* income greater than it was in 1973? Or does your wife have to work to meet the mortgage payments?

Last year companies were "down-sizing" by firing the workers. This year they are "down-sizing" by firing high-level employees. Does that make your stomach churn? Barlett [..] calls it "the dismantling of the middle class".

Do you feel that the U.S.A. has seen its best days, and that your children can expect to have less than you had?

What are the Facts?

In 1950, the United States was the world's fastest-growing nation. In 1992 it ranked *seventh!*[1]

In 1951, U.S. income was the world's highest[2]. In 1992, U. S. wages ranked *ninth!*[3]

The dollar used to be the world's standard currency. Now it is in free-fall.

Government publications[4] list the median family income in constant[5] dollars. This is shown in figure 1. Through the 1950s, 1960s and early '70s our median family income was growing at the rate of 3% per year, but that growth came to a dead stop after 1973. Someone got away with $200 billion per year[6], from productive investment.

Where has that money been going since the 1970s? Read on.

Notes

1. Defined as GDP growth (20 years) per person, corrected for inflation. Ahead of us are Japan, Italy, Germany, Canada, France, and U.K., in that order. *Competitiveness Index* 1994, Council on Competitiveness.
2. McGraw-Hill, message to American Industry. Based on National Product, adjusted for inflation. Canada trailed us by 30%, U.K. by 65% and France by 71%.
3. Ahead of us were Denmark, Switzerland, Norway, Germany, Sweden, Belgium, Canada, and Japan, in that order. Hourly wages, Bank of Austria, *East-West Report Extra,* February 1994.
4. U. S. (1994) *Statistical Abstract of the United States,* Government Printing Office, Washington, DC.
5. "Constant dollars": adjusted to reduce the effects of inflation.
6. In 1993 dollars. Three percent of the 6.4 trillion GDP, rounded.

Bibliography

Barlett, Donald L. and Steele, James B. (1992), *America: What Went Wrong?* (Expanded from a series in the *Philadelphia Enquirer).* Andrews & McMeel.

Bellon, Bertrand and Niosi, Jorge (1988) *The Decline of the American Economy,* Black Rose Books.

Lazitch, Branko (1983,85) *How Democracies Perish* Harper & Row

Phillips, Kevin (1992?) *Boiling Point: Republicans, Democrats, and the Decline of Middle-class Prosperity,* Random House.

Chapter 2
CONGRESSIONAL WASTE

"..When Congress is in session (it's like) when the baby gets hold of a hammer: how much damage he can do before we take it away from him," Will Rogers.

———————

I found out where the missing money went. I followed the Discovery Trail (Appendix A) and it led to Congress.

The Congressional waste is estimated (Page A-5) at about *$195 billion* per year!

How do I know that? The total PAC[1] payments are published: $189 million[2] in 1992. The multiplier for Congress was 1,030 (page A-5). These two numbers multiplied together equal $195 billion.

How Can the Waste be so Great?

It was unexpected that PACs would be so disastrous. The

cause is deviousness. Sometimes a Congressman just grants money to a corporation outright; but most prefer to disguise their spending as a purchase (more details in Appendix A).

What is the Motive for Congress's Spending Frenzy?

Campaign contributions. Friedman[3] wrote that the self-interests of politicians are different from ours.

PACs were started by the labor unions; they always gave money to their favorite candidates[4]. Congress liked that union money and said "Let's get some from industry, too". So they legalized PACs. In 1975 the FEC let down all the bars against corporate money going to Congressmen. "The SUN-PAC decision is easily the most important in the history of the FEC (Federal Elections Commission) and the basis for the rise of corporate PACs" *(Money Talks[5])*. For the whole sad story of the FEC and its "reforms", see *Broken Promise[6]*.

"There is a 'For Sale' sign hanging on the U. S. Capitol," Senator Tim Wirth[7].

The motive is money!

Are Campaign Contributions Bribes?
Definition: bribery is "kicking-back" part of a payment to corrupt an entrusted person. The "kick-back" can occur either after the main payment is received, or before it.

Stern ( ) cites the example of price supports for farm produce. Many of these were initiated in the Depression of the 1930s, but they now are part of "welfare for the rich".

Because they are geared to output, most of this government money is sent "uphill" to the wealthy land-owners. The *poor* farmers don't get much.

Farm price supports are enacted every 5 years, and there have been 30 cycles of "kick-backs" to congressmen in the form of campaign contributions. The candidates know just which lobbyist to look to for money, and how much to expect. They *ask* for money [Clawson pp 59, 115] and often *demand* it [Stern p 164].

If a congressman owes his allegiance to the constituents who elected him and whose money he spends, then Stern showed that voting for farm subsidies is a clear violation of his duty.

Apologists for PAC funding say it is merely supporting the candidates that agree with your objectives. Stern refutes this in his Chapter 8. Much of the milk PAC funding goes to out-of-state legislators who have nothing to do with dairies or farming, many of them from the cities. The PACs are brazenly buying these legislators' votes, and the legislators vote against their constituents [Stern '88 pp 166-8]. The PACs even fund candidates with no opponents [Stern 88 p10]. If that isn't bribery, what is it?

A congressman might say, "I don't take bribes, but my campaign fund could use a donation". In *law* (written by Congress) there is a difference; but in *fact* there is none.

Congressman Javitz (father of the late senator) said that "the only reason (campaign contributions) are not bribery is because Congress defines what bribery is" [Green p 39]. Some Congressmen enrich themselves: "There are virtually no controls on the way campaign money is used" [Clawson p 78].

At least *some* campaign contributions (including PACs) are certainly bribes. Merely giving money the label "campaign fund" does not sanctify it. On several occasions, the courts have ruled that under circumstances existing at the time, the campaign contributions were bribes [Sobel].

For the Voter, Pork-Barrel Economics <u>Does Not</u> Pay!

Brian Kelly wrote "Pork is waste"[8].

You think you're a "free rider"? Remember that the bribe multiplier is 1,030. This means that for every million-dollar contract a legislator brings home to his congressional district, the social cost is about *$1 billion,* and his district's share of the cost is 1/435 of that, or $2.3 million. For each million-dollar contract a *Senator* brings home to his state, the cost to his state is 1/100 of one billion, which equals $10 million. Paying $2.3 million or $10 million to receive a $1 million contract is a bad deal for the people. Don't do me no favors. TANSTAAFL: There Ain't No Such Thing As A Free Lunch (Milton Friedman). Voters *never* get a free ride.

"Bringing home pork" benefits only the congressmen and their paymasters.

Why have the voters put up with it so long?

We Americans have indeed tolerated government corruption far too long. I can think of three possible reasons for this misguided tolerance:
1. It used to be hidden. The USA's tradition of limited government lasted until the 1970s (Appendix E, Fig. 4), when Government Giantism matured; and then the waste was pushed in our face by the S&L collapse of the 1980s.
2. In former years we felt we could do nothing about it anyway. Well, now we can.

3. We are a nation of businessmen, and many of us sell on commission. There is nothing wrong with a salesman sharing in the fruits of his effort.

By analogy, maybe some people accept the idea of *buying* on commission too, as being similar. But nothing could be more wrong!

We want buyers to choose adequate quality at the lowest price. Instead of that, bribes appeal to the buyer's personal enrichment, and his motive is to seek the biggest bribe. He is motivated to bypass competition and to reward inefficient producers, and help them to extend their dead grasp over our economy.

Conclusions:

The growth halt of the 1970s was caused by Congressional waste, motivated by PACs. Both the PACs and the country's economic losses started their escalation in the 1970s. The timing is right, and the amount is right.

Campaign contributions and PACs are bribes, at least in some cases.

Appendix A gives more details on these topics.

Did Anything Else Happen in the 1970s?

Yes, Government Giantism arrived. Government Giantism is discussed in the next chapter.

Notes:

1. PAC, or Political Action Committee: A committee for raising campaign funds. The FEC (Federal Elections Commission) classes PACs as labor, corporate, trade-health-membership, and nonconnected, which are mostly single-issue such as abortion or the environment. The "connected" PACs are an arm of an association or political party, which pays the PAC's expenses and decides where to put its money. [Clawson

et al, *Money Talks*,pp 6-13]
2. Makinson, Larry et al (1994) *Open Secrets: The Encyclopedia of Congressional Money and Politics, 3d Ed.*, p 10, Congressional Quarterly.
3. Friedman, Milton (1993) *Why Government Is The Problem,* Hoover Inst.
4. The labor unions usually favored democrats, but the Teamsters supported Richard Nixon.
5. Clawson, Dan, Neustadtl and Scott (1992) *Money Talks: Corporate PACs and Political Influence,* Harper Collins Basic Books
6. Jackson, Brooks (1990) *Broken Promise: Why the Federal Elections Commission Failed,* 20th Century Fund, Priority Press.
7. Thomas, Bill (1994), *Club Fed: Power, Money, Sex and Violence on Capitol Hill,* Scribner's Sons, p 119.
8. Kelly, Brian (1992), *Adventures in Porkland: How Washington Wastes Your Money and Why They Won't Stop,* Villard Books.

References:
Green, M. with Waldman, M. (1982) *Who Runs Congress?* Dell.
O'Rourke, P. J. *A Parliament of Whores*
Phillips, Kevin (1990) *The Politics of Rich and Poor: Wealth and the American Electorate in the Reagan Aftermath*, Random House.
Phillips, Kevin (1994) *Arrogant Capital: Washington, Wall Street, and the Frustration of American Politics,* Little, Brown.
Sobel, L., ed. (1977) *Corruption in Business,* Facts on File, pp23-33.
Stern, Philip M. (1988) *The Best Congress Money Can Buy*, Random Pantheon.
Stern, Philip M. (1992) *Still the Best Congress Money Can Buy,* Regnery Gateway.
Bibliography:
Atkinson, Rodney (1986) *Government Against the People: The Economics of Political Exploitation,* Compuprint (UK).
Fenwick, Millicent (1982) *Speaking Up*, Harper & Row.
McKinney, Jerome and Johnston, Michael (1986) *Fraud, Waste and Abuse in Government: Causes, Consequences and Cures,* ISHI Pubs.

Chapter 3
GOVERNMENT GIANTISM

"That government is best which governs least," Thomas Jefferson.

Is Bribery a New Thing?

Why is bribery such a problem? Is it a new thing? Certainly not. Bribery is part of traditional politics. (Winter-Berger).

The new thing is Giantism in government.

There are two aspects to giantism in government: (a) the cause(s) of government giantism, and (b) its effect(s) on our economy.

The Causes of Government Giantism

a. *The Money Economy*

In the early 1800s, stock raisers near the upper Ohio River built flatboats to carry their cattle to market in New Orleans, and returned home via the Natchez "trace" (trail). They carried their bag of gold with them; this became known to outlaws along the trail, and some never returned.

Even as late as 1900, most people lived on farms. They subsisted on the land and its products, and on barter. Money was scarce for average people.

Before the money economy, a duke could levy men for an army, promise them plunder, and send them to their death; but they weren't much use to him except in war. Money was so much more attractive to the sovereign because it concentrated the wealth where he could get at it.

Farmers and their property and income were originally fairly safe from the government. You couldn't bribe your congressman with a few bushels of corn -- he had no place to store it.

But there was a limit to what a farmer could do by himself, and as commerce developed it became more profitable to rely on specialists. Shipping made a bigger market for crops, and the farmers could specialize. But canals and then railroads would not barter for their services -- they wanted money. The bigger crop market and specialization provided economies of scale, and this encouraged development of farm machinery. But money was needed to buy the machinery.

The machinery made farm labor more productive. By 1991 only 2.5% of the US population were needed on farms[1] to keep up with our need for food. They were paid money wages.

In this way, even the farmers were drawn into the money economy.

Congress eagerly adapted to the money economy. Congress was launched to make laws, but it changed itself and became the world's biggest spender.

In 1942 Congress struck a huge gusher of money: income tax withholding. This was created as a temporary war emergency measure, but (surprise!) when the war was over, Congress discovered all kinds of "emergencies" and kept it flowing.

At first, the higher brackets of tax were applied to the wealthy, but then inflation took over and the middle class had to pay these rates too[2]. Inflation is a tax on cash.

In 1900, only 7% of our GDP (Gross Domestic Product) was taken by *all* levels of government: federal, state and

local combined. But in 1992, government took between 41%
and 70%[3] of GDP (Figure 4 in Appendix E).

The tax system has grown into a complex monster and
compliance is costly[4]. But Congressmen like it that way
because they can sell relief to their benefactors. Stern wrote
that GE's janitor paid more tax than the Company did.

Conclusion: Our life was transformed by our money
economy. Money was easily seized by the government and
fed its growth.

b.   New Spending Attracts More Campaign Funds

One reason corruption leads to giantism in spending is
that few bribes are offered for continuing old programs.
Each new wave of politicians invents new agendas for
spending and "sells" its own new excuses.

Usually the old spending is kept on because its
beneficiaries now have vested interests[5]: the "iron triangle[2]".
The new spending just gets added-on, without end. This
causes government to grow into new areas of life.

The President spent much of 1994 vainly "selling"
Universal Health Care to the country. Health care already
costs us 14% of GDP; imagine how the cost would grow
with more government in it!

The Effects of Government Giantism

The other reason that government spending became more
important in the 1970s was, that's when it got big enough to
make a difference. Before that (except for World War II),
governments took so little of the GDP that the tribute
amounted only to a small burden on the economy. But in
1975 spending by the government (all levels) reached 35 to
54%[3] of the GDP, so government waste now became

important to the economy.

Government spending appears to inhibit economic growth[6].

Conclusions:

There are two things to be said about government giantism:

(a)   ***Causes of giantism:*** Government giantism ***results from*** the money economy and the spreading of government into new areas, and

(c)   ***Effect of giantism:*** Government waste became our greatest economic problem only after government giantism arrived.

Notes:

1. *World Almanac.*
2. Friedman, Milton and Rose (1983) *Tyranny of the Status Quo,* Harcourt Brace Jovanovitch, pp 40-8.
3. Figure 4 of Appendix E. The range of values is intended to cover all assumed values for the Productivity of government spending. This is explained in Appendix E.
4. Payne, James L. (1993) *Costly Returns: The Burdens of the U. S. Tax System,* ICS Press.
5. Consider Social Security, for example. There are arguments for and against Old Age and Survivors Insurance; but for most retired people it is an essential part of their income, and they feel very strongly that they have ***earned*** it.
6. Landau, Daniel (1983), Government Expenditure and Economic Growth, *Southern Economic Journal,* v 49, pp 783-92. Also:

Carr, Jack (1989), Government Size and Economic Growth, *American Econ. Rev.* v 79 pp 267-71.

Stern, Philip M. (1988) *The Best Congress Money Can Buy,* Pantheon (Random House), p 10.

Chapter 4
CORRUPTION SCHOOL

One should not look too closely at how sausages or laws or made
(Bismarck).

———————

Candidates appeal to the voters by promising to "clean up Washington". And a few of them even mean it. The "reform" refrain was louder than ever in the elections of 1992 and 1994. But after the new freshmen arrived in Congress, they changed. The words are different but the wasteful spending goes on. We need to know why, and Bill Thomas, the veteran Beltway newsman tells us in a humorous book about our National Tragedy: Congress.

How do good citizens get to be so bad? They go to school.

In the roaring 1980s, the HUD (Housing and Urban Development) corruption scandal, the Savings and Loan collapse and other capers of Democratic Congresses and Republican Presidents had brazenly plundered the nation's economy. In 1992 and -94, the voters' rebellion ended both the Republican presidency and the Democratic Congress. The new Republicans in Congress ("freshmen") met in Omaha and issued a shock-therapy manifesto calling for a ban on PAC contributions and an end to the seniority system.

The new class of freshmen was typecast as a wrecking crew, but the political bosses were ready for them with "Freshmen Orientation", the incumbent-defense plan.

Their first two weeks on Capitol Hill were taken up with banquets and lectures by the old-time committee chairmen.

There were even lectures on **ethics,** where they were taught the difference between campaign contributions and bribery. "Don't accept payment for any service where the Federal Government is involved." "But you **can** vote for things to enhance your financial well-being." The freshmen could understand this kind of hair-splitting, because 48 of them were lawyers. But "there are virtually no controls on the way campaign money is used" [Clawson p 78].

After the initial Capitol Hill lectures, the Democrat tradition since 1972 was to attend lectures at Harvard's John F. Kennedy School's Institute of Politics, to learn why we **should** have deficit spending [Thomas p 107].

But the new Republican power rebelled at that and sponsored conservative lectures at Annapolis. New Democrat members were forbidden by their bosses to attend these, and none did.

Legislators have two motives: to get elected, and to get reelected. Legislators have the power to spend billions, but that spending power depends on allegiance to party objectives and the established chain of command, and on being assigned to spending committees. Members of the club have to "go along to get along" (logrolling, vote trading: if you'll vote for my pork, I'll vote for yours).

Brian Kelly related what happened to the "Porkbusters" in 1991 (pp 197-200).

The freshmen came there to change the system, but three weeks later they *were* the system. They were "terminally congressionalized", "Gingrichized" and "Gephardtified".

Conclusion:
Freshman Orientation is a school where Congress teaches its form of corruption.

References
Bailey, F. G. (1988) *Humbuggery and Manipulation: The Art of Leadership,* Cornell U. Pr.
Baker, Ross K. (1989) *The New Fat Cats: Members of Congress as Political Benefactors,* 20th Century Fund, Priority Press Publications.
Clawson, Dan, Neustadtl and Scott (1992) *Money Talks: Corporate PACs and Political Influence,* Harper Collins Basic Books.
Kelly, Brian (1992) *Adventures in Porkland: How Washington Wastes Your Money and Why They Won't Stop.* Villard.
Thomas, Bill (1994) *Club Fed: Power, Money, Sex and Violence on Capitol Hill,* Charles Scribner's Sons.

Bibliography:
Birnbaum, Jeffrey H. (1992) *The Lobbyists: How Influence Peddlers Get Their Way in Washington*, Times Books.

Chapter 5
THE CURE

"The price of liberty is eternal vigilance."
John Philpot Curran and Thomas Jefferson.

———————

The new Republican Congress promises to balance the budget in seven years. That same promise has been going around for thirty years. If you believe it I have a nice bridge to sell you.

But **something** has to be done. Too many people have discovered how to raid the treasury through Congress.

The voters are disgusted with their choices on election day. They stay away in droves.

Would you like to have more income and more job security?

Would you like for your government to be efficient and caring?

Would you like to see it move from seventh place in economic growth, back to *first* place?

Of course you would. I would too.

Well now you can make government more efficient.

The Cure
Ted Van Dyk wrote "How to clean up ... Eliminate PACs".

The cure is to stop corruption and bribery.

But how? Not by legislation. Since the beginning of time, *all* candidates for office have promised to clean up politics, but they never do. They don't refuse that money.

Congressmen are in Washington because we voters put them there -- we elected them.

The ***voter's revenge*** is to vote bribe-takers out of office.

I may be cheated, but I don't have to vote for the cheaters!

How will you know a bribe-taker when you see one? Are there any congressmen who don't take bribes? Yes, a few. Project Vote Smart (page 26) or Makinson [p 20] will tell you In the 1992 election, 26 (5%) of the congressmen (Democrats and Republicans) refused PAC funds[1]:

Bill Archer	Peter Hoekstra	Romano Mazzoli
Scotty Baesler	Martin Hoke	Martin Meehan
Anthony Bellenson	Steve Horn	William Natcher
David Boren	Michael Huffington	Glenn Poshard
Jim Cooper	Andrew Jacobs	Ralph Regula
Philip Crane	Herb Kohl	Nick Smith
Terry Everett	Jim Leach	Mike Synar
Bill Goodling	Edward Merkey	Peter Torkildsen
Bill Gradison		

Which path?

American economic life is at a fork in the road. It could go in either of two directions:

1.   Straight ahead, with politics as usual spending and wasting more than half the GDP. As we waste our capital, Kennedy[3] and Jacobs[4] predict the future of our decline. We will need to face up to our third-world future and stop being the world's sugar-daddy and the world's policeman; or

2.   Back to 1900, when the spending of *all* governments (federal, state and local) was only 7% of GDP.

I prefer the middle path.

What Is Our Objective?

We can improve our politics by rooting out bribery wherever we find it.

1.   To clean the financial vandals and the buccaneers out of positions of political power;

2.   To return to government the traditions of George Washington, who was offered and refused a third term as president, and of Thomas Jefferson, who said that government is best which governs least.

There are a lot of selfish legislators around -- the money attracts them like flies. And there are lots of good, public-spirited people. We need to trade-in the first for the second.

To Stop the Waste, How Should You Vote?

Vote for the candidates who have taken no PAC money.

If all candidates are taking PAC money, then vote for the candidate who takes the least.

If all candidates *were* taking PAC money in the past, then vote for the first candidate who quit taking it.

If the candidate takes money for a cause that you agree with, you can vote for him/her. But don't vote for a candidate just because he brings "pork" home to your state. Chapter 2 shows that that does not work!

When in doubt, vote against the incumbent. He is hard to unseat, because incumbents get the most PAC money. Maybe a 3/4 majority should be required to reelect an incumbent.

Vote against the incumbents who spent the most money.

When in doubt, vote against the candidate you heard the most about. He probably spent the most money on advertising himself.

If a candidate is rich and using his own money, how did

he earn it? What matters is not whether he is rich or poor. What matters is if he intends to *get* rich on plunder; then we need to vote against him. If he got rich in politics, watch out!

When in doubt, don't vote; it dilutes the informed votes.

How NOT to vote:

The one who is presented on the TV talk-show as the handsomest, the glibbest, the one who wins the debates.

Don't be Taken-in by these sob-stories -- ignore them:

The need for more campaign funds. Of course, so long as most candidates accept PAC money. But the cure is not to give them more PAC money, or government money. The cure is to abolish PAC money. The legislators will never do that; only the voters can. After the PAC money is gone, elections will cost less.

Lobbyists are needed for information on the issues: nonsense. If the legislator can't understand it by himself and with his 40 assistants, he should not be spending our money for it.

Congress's bills *are* incomprehensible[5], but they are cleverly written that way to hide their real purpose[2].

Some legislators take all the bribes that are offered them. Then when they get caught with their hand in the cookie jar, they give back one cookie so they look sanctimonious. Committees of their fellow members accept this nonsense, but voters should not.

Party loyalty: Both political parties have a ritual that comes around as regular as the seasons: After all the name-calling and mud-slinging for the primary elections, the sweet refrain is "All is forgiven. Come back home -- your party needs you."

Forget party loyalty. This is a national emergency.

Can government be improved, as Peters thinks it might? Well, we can find out. The first step is to reject the bribe-takers, and then the bribe-*givers* will disappear. Then we can take on the vote-traders.

Can something be done? Can the leaks be stopped? You bet.

The voters have complete control. To take back their government and their economy, all they need to do is to forget party loyalty and vote out bribe-takers.

Do we know more about politics than previous generations did? I wonder. The "realities" of politics are not taught in *our* schools, because the business-booster PACs won't let them. I was taught the "realities" of politics by my father and grandfather. They would never vote for any candidate who they knew had taken bribes.

Notes:

1. Makinson, Larry (1994) *Open Secrets*: The Cash Constituents of Congress, Center for Responsive Politics, Congressional Quarterly. This is a 362-page digest of *Open Secrets: The Encyclopedia of Congressional Money and Politics,* (3d edition), 1,362 pages. Both are published in even years.
2. Clawson, Dan, Neustadtl, Alan and Scott, Denise, (1992) *Money Talks: Corporate PACs and Political Influence,* HarperCollins BasicBooks.
3. Kennedy, Paul (1987) *The Rise and Fall of the Great Powers: Economic Change and Military Conflict from 1500 to 2000,* Random House,p514.

4. Jacobs, Jane (1985) *Cities & the Wealth of Nations: Principles of Economic Life,* Random. Also "The Dynamic of Decline" (1984) *Atlantic Monthly,* April, pp 98 -114.
5. Richardson, Senator H. L. ("Bill") (1978) *What Makes You Think We Read the Bills?* Green Hill, Caroline House.

References:
Peters, Charles (1993), How Washington Really Works, *Washington Monthly,* Jan/Feb, pp43 +.

Chapter 6
THE CONSEQUENCES

"Damn the torpedoes - Full speed ahead!" Farragut, Mobile Bay, 1864.

I hope this book will start a peaceful revolution.

I'm sure there are some well-meaning congressmen. Maybe they just *don't know* how much damage they are doing. This book provides new information, and it may encourage some congressmen to spend our money more carefully.

Voting this way would certainly impact Washington, and the results could be startling. Congress would no longer be a place to get rich quick[1]. Washington's 4,000 PACs [Thomas p. 116] can close their doors, and the lobbyists will leave Washington like ticks from a dead dog. The University course in lobbying[2] can be discontinued.

Many people who make a living at the public trough may have to find another career. New Zealand is ahead of us in abolishing farm price supports: it took seven years for agriculture to adjust, but it's better off[3].

Bribery needs to recover its former status of social stink.

The tax burden will drop, the economy will soar again, and good jobs will be plentiful. Best of all, the government will be more *efficient, effective* and *responsive,* to do those things that only government can do well. The waste will be cut from colossal to manageable.

Until that happy day, we are better-off keeping as much money as possible away from Congress.

Can we make government so clean that we can go ***more*** socialist (on health care, for example)? The trouble is, Appendix C shows that adding more layers of planning and interference degrades efficiency. We can wait and see how efficient government is without bribery.

Will this solve all political problems? Of course not. But bribery is the first problem. If bribery can be recognized for what it is, we won't have office-holders bending all their efforts toward lining their own pockets, and the waste that goes with it; and crooks will be less attracted to positions of power.

If we ***don't*** do something, we'll go down the tubes, because government is threatening more spending all the time.

After scrubbing out PAC bribery, we can get to the next problem, which is vote-trading (another form of bribery [Stern, Thomas]).

Look for the next edition of this book in 1997. I might make mistakes, but one thing is sure: I'll never lie to you.

Notes:

1. Bank robber Willie Sutton, when asked why he robbed banks, replied "That's where the money is." Well, now it's in Congress.

2. Bandow, Doug (1990) *The Politics* of Plunder: Misgovernment in Washington, Transaction Pubs., p 52.

3. *Economist*, (1994) Don't Wait until the Cows Come Home, v325, Dec. 12, pS14.

4. Stern, Philip M. (1988) *The Best Congress Money Can Buy,* Pantheon, Random House, pp 84-7.

5. Thomas, Bill (1994) *Club Fed: Power, Money, Sex and Violence on Capitol Hill,* Charles Scribner's Sons p 91+.

Additional Reading:

American Institute of Economic Research, Great Barrington, MA 01230.

Center for Responsive Politics, Congressional Quarterly, 1414 22d St. NW, Washington, DC 20037.

CATO Institute, 1000 Massachusetts Ave. NW, Washington, DC 20001-5403.

Common Cause magazine, 2030 M St. NW, Washington, DC 20036.

Liberty, Box 1181, Port Townsend, WA 98368.

Mother Jones, 731 Market St. Suite 600, San Francisco, CA 94103.

Project Vote Smart, Center for National Independence in Politics, 129 NW 4th St. #204, Corvallis, OR 97330.

Public Citizen magazine, 2000 P St. NW, Suite 600, Washington, DC 20036.

Reason magazine, 3415 S. Sepulveda Blvd. Suite 400, Los Angeles, CA 90034.

Washington Monthly magazine, 1611 Connecticut Ave. NW, Washington, DC 20009.

Appendix A
THE TRAIL OF DISCOVERY

"A cynic sees things as they are, not as they ought to be."
Ambrose Bierce.

————————

I have always been interested in efficient production on the one hand, and confidence games and scams on the other hand; and I have been collecting source materials on them for decades.

One type of corruption is bribery.

A bribe is a gift or promise offered for wrongful favors in violation of duty or trust. In buying, "kick-backs" to the buyer or agent are reported frequently.

I wanted to find out the costs, or losses associated with bribery. I wished to quantify its effects, so I adopted a ratio for this: the PAC multiplier[1,2].

However, bribery is not an easy thing to research, because the people who do bribery try to hide it. So I used an indirect method: I sought out those cases where the money spent was a *total* loss and calculated the ratio of the cost to the bribe. This ratio is a ***multiplier*** for bribes.

There are all kinds of studies about the economics of the country, but there are few studies on bribery. When bribery *is* studied, it is often excused; bribes are thought to be only a small fraction of the economy[3].

But I found that the cost of bribery is much greater than the amount of the bribe, because of the deviousness used to hide the bribery, and because bribes are used to avoid free and open competition.

The Cost of Bribery
I studied bribery and wrote the cases up in a paper titled *The Cost of Bribery,* intended for an academic journal. The paper was not popular: I eventually approached 40 editors. The first 39 editors did not want to see any criticism of bribery. Maybe the professors are afraid of losing their government grants.

That first paper[4] studied bribery in random places and circumstances.

As one example, in the 1930s a state insurance superintendent refunded $8 million of impounded funds, in return for a bribe of $½ million cash paid in a hotel room in Kansas City, Mo[5]. In this case the multiplier was 16: that is, to "earn" his bribe of $½ million, he defrauded the policy holders of 16 times that much.

This study taught me several lessons:

1.   One thing I learned was that bribery always has a *victim*. Where the bribery involved some level of government, the victim was usually the public.

2.   Bribery requires a conspiracy between at least two people: (a) the person controlling the treasury or other valuables, and (b) the bribe-*giver*, who is the main beneficiary of the scheme.

3.   Bribery is a costly way of doing business.

And that is the whole point of my case against bribery. In corrupt circumstances, a dictator can just reach into the safe and *take* the money that he controls. In that case, the cost would equal the loot and the multiplier would be one. But in a democracy with a free press, the leaders prefer to "cover-up" their theft by devious actions[6]. This cover-up usually requires that corrupt leaders misdirect the money entrusted to them into corrupt channels; then they get only a fraction of the money because their fellow conspirators want some of the loot. Additional loss is caused by inefficiency in production and purchasing, because the bribe shelters these processes from competition.

For the random bribery cases I studied first, the multiplier had a median value of about 15. But that study deliberately excluded the Savings and Loan failures of the 1980s, because their full story was just beginning to come out at that time.

In 1993 I studied the GDP (Gross Domestic Product). It is calculated by adding-in all government spending. I had just discovered lots of waste in government spending, so it seemed to me that this method of calculation would give an optimistic result (biased on the high side). [Carr] concurs with that. This study is included as Appendix E in this book.

The Savings & Loan Collapse of the 1980s

Next, I studied the S&L cases, and these were instructive. The S&Ls had several serious problems: (a) government insurance on bank and S&L deposits (the "moral hazard"); (b) a series of shocks to the economy; (c) a supply of cash-hungry real estate speculators, and (d) a corrupt congressman who headed the banking committee.

The first shock to the economy was a successful move by the oil cartel (OPEC) to limit production and drive up oil prices. This led to inflation and hardship for the S&Ls.

In the 1970s and early 1980s, congress and the regulators went for the cash[7,8,9] in the S&Ls. The Associations specified what they wanted: (a) more depositor insurance, and (b) deregulation; and they paid for these in campaign contributions.

Deregulation was the policy of both parties -- democratic and republican politicians. Under its trendy rubric, Congress opened the S&Ls to real estate developers and other money-hungry high-flyers.

In 1974 new Federal rules permitted "conversion" of S&Ls, from ownership by at least 400 depositors (the previous rule), to ownership by almost anyone including real estate developers and speculators[10].

Deposit insurance was bloated far beyond the average depositor's needs. In 1974, insurance was increased to $40,000 per account, and in 1980 it was again increased to $100,000 per account [Barth]. This was more than ten times greater than the need of the average depositor.

The reckless new owners of the "go-go" S&Ls were gamblers, especially on sure things. It is an ancient scam to gamble with someone else's money: it's called "heads I win, tails you lose."

(a) They attracted "deposit brokers" by offering recklessly high rates of interest, and there was no risk to the S&L because of the government insurance. The OPEC countries stuffed their huge cartel profits into U.S. banks and S&Ls, and these deposit brokers were the pipeline.

There were corrupt deposit brokers who demanded "kick-backs" for making deposits in the S&L.

(b) Many of the new S&L owners were real estate developers and speculators. The money-stuffing by deposit brokers into the S&Ls encouraged gambling with their depositors' money. Unwise lending[11] (often to themselves, or in distant states) caused a real estate boom.

The more unscrupulous S&Ls performed frequent land "flips", to inflate the price and to "earn" fees. The more reckless S&Ls got rid of their own in-house property assessors and contracted-out to those assessors who gave them the "correct" (inflated) estimates.

So the S&Ls gambled in two ways: on the interest they paid for brokered deposits, and on their sham profits in real estate[8].

The money-stuffing by deposit brokers also encouraged lending to third-world countries (on "commission"), many of which defaulted, leading to a banking crisis.

Only a few of the S&Ls went really "bad", but deregulation made it an unstable situation: in the real estate "bubble" with its sham paper "profits", small S&Ls bought for trifles by reckless speculators grew to be among the largest in the nation (on paper).

The result was over-valued real estate and a wave of S&L failures in the 1980s. This amounted to a raid on the U.S. treasury, because the treasury took the losses, not the depositors.

What was the Motive for S&L Deregulation?

The S&L collapse caught Congress red-handed and red-faced. Why did Congress do it? What was their motive?

The most influential figure in deregulation of the S&Ls was the chairman of the House Banking Committee, Fernand St Germain of Rhode Island. He should have been "minding the store", but he was actually being paid-off by the "bad" ("high-flier") S&Ls to do what they wanted[7]. Some of these pay-offs were campaign contributions funneled through the S&L Association PACs. What they wanted was more Deposit Insurance, S&L "conversion" to greedy ownership (mostly by real estate developers), and "forbearance" from regulators for "zombie" S&Ls, and they got it. That is clear from Jackson's book[7]. According to Jackson's and Stern's accounts, this can be judged bribery. Indeed, St Germain's corruption scandal lost him the 1988 election.

The motive was bribery -- bribery in congress and bribery permitted by congress.

Bribery in the form of PAC money and other campaign contributions was the cause of the S&L failures. The same shocks hit the banks, but *they* survived.

Throughout the government, deregulation was in the air. How much of this political environment was *itself* caused by bribery is not known to me, but bribery *did* cause the S&L collapse.

I wrote an academic article called *The Cost of Bribery and Self-Dealing in the S&L Failures*[8], accepted for publication in 1995.

My studies had shown that bribery costs the public much more than the amount of the bribe. How much more?

Where congressmen were involved in the S&L failures, the multiplier was a shocker: about *15,000!*[8]

For several days I went around in a daze, marveling at this monstrous multiplier. The Savings and Loan disaster had uncovered the biggest cause of our economic decay: Congress. The Congressmen seem to treat the billions they are trusted with like play money. No wonder this country was having economic troubles: a good chunk of our wealth had been sold or given away by Congress.

Conclusion:

The corruption in congress did not begin with PACs, but the S&L failures exposed the cost of Congress's bribery game.

The Cost/PAC Multiplier for Congress

Did this horrendous multiplier apply only to the Savings and Loan failures, or was it true also for other acts of Congress?

To answer that question I did a third study, this time on Congress. This study is included in this book as Appendix D.

Congress is a difficult subject to research, because Congressmen hide their "pork". "Pork" spending is piously disguised as Spending for Good Causes, for example foreign aid, education, a dam, or an aircraft carrier, and who can tell their actual value? There is certainly venality in defense contracting, for example, but it is ambiguous: who can we trust to estimate the real value to society of an aircraft carrier? This question could lead to an endless ideological wrangle. It depends on who you listen to.

Congress's Price Supports on Farm Produce

Appendix D is mostly about farm price supports. Price supports take two main forms: (a) subsidies, or price guarantees, and (b) restrictions on supply, including import restrictions. These supports started in the 1930s depression, to help poor farmers, but times have changed. Now the big farms control the market, and their owners are no longer poor.

If you are feeling sympathy for the farmers, don't. There are still farmers in poverty, but farming is a business. The public doesn't support grocery stores or filling stations; why should it support farmers?

Price supports are paid to the *owners* of farms, not to the workers. Bovard estimated that the average full-time farmer has a net worth of $822,000. The farm subsidy programs pump money "uphill": they take money from the consumers and taxpayers (including the poor) and give it to the rich [Bovard].

Many of these subsidies have now become "allotments". They have become detached from the land and are now owned by non-farmers. Many of the largest government checks go to New York City and Beverly Hills, California. Eighty percent of the tobacco fields are in this category. One arm of government pays for growing tobacco, while another arm spends for propaganda against its use. Efficiency?

Are Farm PACs bribes?

Recall the definition: a bribe is a gift or promise offered for wrongful favors *in violation of duty or trust*. Bribery is "kicking-back" part of a payment to corrupt the person entrusted to spend it.

About 75% of the government benefits go to the largest 25% of the farms, which don't need them [Sanderson p 3]. These 75% are *wrongful* payments.

To whom does a congressmen owe his allegiance? Where does his duty lie?

He owes his allegiance to the voters, and he is entrusted to spend their money for their benefit. Party and PAC money are bribes if they cause the legislator to violate his duty.

The legislators have different motives than the voters do [Friedman]. The frantic search for money for the *next* election campaign starts on the first day in office and conflicts with that rightful allegiance to the voters and taxpayers [Thomas p 113]. The legislator's incentive is to do what the PACs want done; and continual fund-raising leaves him little time for other activities. Candidates are relying on corporate PACs so much that they are unable to represent the interests of ordinary citizens [Cabot].

The farm PACs support legislators who vote subsidies for farmers; the sugar PACs support those who vote benefits for sugar, dairy for dairy, etc. Welch found a correlation between votes and dairy payments. There is a cycle of payments from farmers to legislators alternating with payments by legislators to farmers, and this cause-and-effect cycle has repeated itself over and over through 30 election cycles, (nearly 100 cycles for sugar). The farmers "kick-back" to the legislators (through PACs) a small part of the funds they receive from the treasury. [Stern] wrote that Congressmen in non-farming states were induced to vote *against* the interests of their constituents, who pay more for food.

Farm PACs are unequivocal: Congress gives dollars to the farm owners, in exchange for dollars of campaign contributions, at the exchange rate of 4,000 for one! The transaction is strictly cash both ways, and the farmers could never find a greater return on their investment!

Giving away the public's money to a few wealthy supporters *is* "in violation of duty". Thus farm PACs appear to be pure bribes.

Abler[12] studied logrolling (vote trading -- another form of bribery) in farm legislation.

Are _ALL_ PACs bribes?

Congress says no, campaign contributions are not bribery. But this can be ignored as self-serving.

Senator Bob Dole said [Stern '88 p 77] "When these PACs give money, they expect something in return other than good government." But Senator Dole's money-raising from ADM, sugar, tobacco (in *Kansas?*) and commodity traders is told by Stern, pp 77-88.

I don't know the answer -- I have not studied all PACs. I *have* studied two types of PACs: S&L PACs and Farm PACs, and both were bribes.

Snyder[14] distinguishes between "Ideological" and "Investor" PACs and he writes of "investment" in politicians, by means of PAC funds. This investment is speculative; some candidates don't make it into office. But the returns have been great. Appendix D reports a Return on Investment (ROI) of more than 1,000-to-one (sec. 3.3). Stratmann[13] concluded that logrolling was more influential than ideology.

"Striking correlations are found between Congressional votes and

PAC contributions from interest groups" [Cabot p 12]. "Elected officials no longer try to carry out the will of the people or to 'maximize' their interests. Money must be spent on interest groups to keep reelection funds coming to politicians" [Brusca].

"Money unquestionably is the most debilitating and corrupting force in American politics today" [Demaris p 371].

"A candidate ... is imprisoned (by debt) before he ever reaches Congress" [Drew p 94].

"The twilight zone between bribery and legitimate campaign contributions has become even more indistinguishable" [Loeb p 98].

Republican Congressman Jim Leach, of Iowa said, "What you've done is turn upside-down the American premise of government, which is the idea that people are elected to represent people. Officeholders should be indebted to the individuals that cast the ballots. Today candidates are becoming increasingly indebted to the people that *influence* the people who cast the ballots. ... prohibit group giving, period." [Stern p 145]

"So who rules Congress? ... Cash. Members are run by the special interests who enable them to run for office. ... he who has the gold, rules" [Green p 159].

To what extent do legislators "sell" their office for money?

Senator Phil Gramm's Funding-Scare Strategy *[Bill Thomas]:*

"Once assured that a federal project was in absolutely no danger of having its funding cut, Gramm's staff would leak word to the Texas media that the project was in serious danger, and only swift and decisive action by Gramm could save it." The backers would contribute, "Gramm would pretend to throw his weight around in Washington, and the funding would be 'restored' and a community rescued from the brink of disaster." This happened with Brooke Army Medical Hospital Center in San Antonio in Gramm's 1990 reelection bid. The Dallas Morning News broke the story three years later.

Why our Economic Growth Stopped

Chapter 1 estimated that since the 1970s, $200 billion per year (1993 dollars) had been diverted from productive channels. Where did that wealth go? What happened in the 1970s?

What happened was that Congress "reformed" campaign financing. It declared that bribery was now legal[15].

Does it add up? Does the social cost of congressional bribery match the development shortfall of $200 billion?

The total amount of Congress's campaign finance bribes in 1992 was $189 million (Makinson). The social cost can be found by multiplying this number by the PAC multiplier for congress. That multiplier is calculated in the "Appendix to this Appendix" (page A-10); It is 1,030. Multiplying yields (1,030)x($189 million) = $195 billion.

The Numbers Match!

This is a good match to the $200 billion that was found missing in Chapter 1.

In fact, the closeness of the match is partly luck, considering that:
(a) the PAC multiplier is known only to a crude approximation as yet (page D-7), and
(b) I used the farm multiplier to estimate the cost for *all* acts of Congress.
This is a new kind of statistic, in a field where people try to hide their acts. But this multiplier is so important to the economy that even a rough estimate is better than ignorance. This is the best data I have, so I use it. I hope that future research will produce more accurate data.

The waste-to-loot principle.

But the worst is yet to come. Congressional "bills" are undecipherable (Chapter 5), so if bribed congressmen receive a "commission" (campaign contribution) on their spending, why bother to spend intelligently? Why not just waste the money? Brian Kelly says that indeed they do: "Pork is waste". He classifies pork spending in the following categories (pp 201-225):

Rotten Pork	Perpetual Pork	Culture Pork
Power Pork	Presidential Pork	Subsidy Pork
Charity Pork	Academic Pork	Byrd Pork

Trophy Pork   Sneaky Pork   Tax Pork
Defense Pork   Greasy Pork (p 150)

Lobbying for foreign countries:
When I worked overseas in the third world, it seemed that U. S. loans just disappeared into the maw of the local government. When the time came to repay them, it was like giving loans to your family: you are a Scrooge if you insist on repayment. So Congress loans them money to pay the *interest,* throwing good money after bad. [Bandow] recites the horrors of finance in Zaire.

Congress is still giving money away to foreign countries. Our growth is heading for third-world status, but Congress is still doing first-world spending and lending.

What motivates this frenzy for Congress to send money out of the country?

One answer could be -- **CONSULTING FEES!** Deposited in offshore banks, tax-free! For bribe-takers, gifts, loans and favors to foreign governments are especially attractive, because they are shielded from exposure by international boundaries. At the end of this Appendix is a bibliography on foreign lobbies.

Appendix

The Farm PAC Multiplier
I found that the median multiplier for farm PACs was 4,127 (Appendix D, Section 4) -- not as great as in the S&L cases, but still very serious. Because 3/4 of these payments went to "enrich the rich", the waste/PAC multiplier is $(4,127) \times (3/4) = 3,095$.

Is this cost a social waste? That depends. It could be argued that the rich looters return their loot to the economy in high living, but that is not always true -- much of it goes into offshore bank accounts. In either case it is often mis-directed, that is, not invested in the growth of the U.S. economy.

Such a high multiplier is almost incredible. It could be understood if there were a long chain of conspirators, each expecting his "cut" of the loot. But with farm price supports, the "chain" has only two links: legislation, and PACs.

The reason for a high multiplier is that bribery motivates give-aways, needless spending, and buying from wasteful or exploitative sources. Olson wrote that special-interest groups reduce efficiency. Myrdal wrote that obstruction or delay can be used to extort bribes; such tactics are totally counter-productive and are inherently wasteful.

In the case of farm price supports, there is another source of waste, as far as U.S. income and growth are concerned. Subsidized prices, as in the case of milk and sugar, are intended to benefit U.S. producers, but they do this only indirectly. Much of their benefit goes to foreign producers instead. The "transfer efficiency" to the domestic producers was only 1/3 (Section 3.2 of Appendix D), so the waste was 2/3 the above number, or about 2,062.

The Farm PAC Multiplier for Congress

For Congress, the PAC multiplier, or bribe multiplier found above was 3,095. This is based mostly on farm price subsidies.

Bribery may not have been the sole cause, so we take ½ of the above multiplier (Section 3.1 of Appendix D), or about 1,550.

To recap this calculation:

Median PAC multiplier from Table 1, Appendix D:	4,127
Allowance for possible shared cause:	x 0.5
Benefits wasted (enriching the rich):	x 0.75
Transfer inefficiency	x 2/3
Estimated (waste)/(PAC total):	1,030

Notes:

1. I originally called it the cost/bribe ratio. "PAC multiplier" seems simpler.
2. This book explains the 1970s halt in our economic growth as caused by PACs. But I did not start out that way; the bribery study was independent. Only after I estimated the loss due to bribery, did I make the connection with the halt in growth.
3. About 1%: estimate by the Washington Post in 1976. Reisman, W. M. (1979) *Folded Lies: Bribery, Crusades and Reforms.* The Free Press (MacMillan).
4. Brooks, Herb (1993), The Cost of Bribery, *Human Systems*

Management, v 12 pp 205-210, IOS Press.

5. Kohn, G. C. (1989), *Encyclopedia of American Scandal,* Facts on File.

6. This might imply that the bribe multiplier is greater in democracies than in dictatorships. What I suspect is that **all** the world's big governments are still primitive and corrupt.

Even with corrupt government, our country was great until government grew too big. It may be that after a country's government grows to giantism the nation is hopelessly inefficient without noble leadership. Maybe the only way for a country to remain strong is to (a) keep its government small, or (b) keep its leadership in noble hands. This is what I want our voters to do, and a democracy offers more freedom for them to do it. We are very fortunate that we have a free press -- many countries do not.

I have no data on whether dictatorships are more efficient than democracies, so I leave that question for others to study. I hope the answer is "no" -- I don't want to live in a dictatorship. But I suspect the democratic governments need to be further developed and specially defended against corruption.

7. Jackson, Brooks (1990), *Honest Graft: Big Money and the American Political Process,* Farragut.

8. Brooks, Herb (1995), The Cost of Bribery and Self-Dealing in the S&L Failures, *Human Systems Management,* IOS Press.

9. Like Willie Sutton. When Sutton was asked why he robbed banks, he replied: "That's where the money is."

10. Waldman, Michael (1990), *Who Robbed* America? A Citizen's Guide to the Savings & Loan Scandal, Random House, p 21.

11. Chapter 3 shows that the waste goes with the bribes, because of deviousness.

12. Abler, David G. (1989), Vote Trading on Farm Legislation in the U. S. House, *American Agricult. Economics Assn,* v71, Aug pp 583-91.

13. Stratmann, Thomas (1992) The Effects of Logrolling on Congressional Voting, *The American Economic Review,* v82, No5 pp1162-1176.

14. Snyder, James M. Jr. (1992) Long-term Investing in Politicians; or, Give Early, Give Often, *Journal of Law and Economics,* v XXXV, Apr.

15. Clawson, Dan, Neustadtl and Scott (1992) *Money Talks: Corporate*

PACs and Political Influence, Harper Collins Basic Books.

Other References:
Barth, J.T. (1991) The Great Savings & Loan Debacle, AEI Press.

Bovard, James (1991), *The Farm Fiasco: How Federal Agriculture Policy Squanders Billions of Dollars a Year, Sacrifices the Poor to the Rich, and Gives Congressmen and Bureaucrats vast Arbitrary Power over American Citizens,* ICS Press, p 50.

Brusca (1990) *Financial World,* Dec. 11.

Carr, Jack L. (1989), "Government Size and Economic Growth," *Amer Econ Rev,* v 79 pp 267-71.

Cabot, E. and Sheekey, K. (1990), PACs are Bad News for Democracy, *Across the Board,* v 27 p11(3) December.

Demaris, O (1974) *Dirty Business: The Corporate-Political Money-Power Game,* Harper & Row, p 371. Also pp185-8.

DioGuardi, Joseph (1992) *Unaccountable Congress: It Doesn't Add Up,* Regnery Gateway. DioGuardi is especially well-qualified. He is a CPA, former Congressman, and founder of **Truth in Government**.

Drew, Elizabeth (1983) *Politics and Money: The New Road to Corruption*, MacMillan.

Friedman, Milton (1993) *Why Government is the Problem,* Hoover Inst.

Kelly, Brian (1992) *Adventures in Porkland: How Washington Wastes Your Money and Why They Won't Stop.* Villard Books.

Loeb, L (1975) *American Politics,* MacMillan.

Myrdal, Gunnar (1978) *Corruption: Its Causes and Effects,* Chapt. 55 in Heidenheimer, pp 540-5, esp. 541.

Olsen, Mancur (1982) *The Rise and Decline of Nations: Economic Growth, Stagflation, and Social Rigidities,* Yale U. Pr.

Sanderson, Fred H., editor (1990), *Agricultural Protectionism in the Industrialized World,* Resources for the Future.

Stern, Philip M. (1988) *The Best Congress Money Can Buy,* Pantheon, Random House.

Stern, Philip M. (1992) *Still The Best Congress Money Can Buy.* Regnery Gateway, chapter 8.

Thomas, Bill (1994) *Club Fed: Power, Money Sex and Violence on Capitol Hill,* Charles Scribner's Sons, pp 29-31.

Bibliography on Foreign Aid
Bandow, Doug (1990) *The Politics of Plunder: Misgovernment in Washington,* Transaction Pub., p 487-8.
Boulton, D (1978) *The Grease Machine,* Harper & Row
Choate, Pat (1990) *Agents of Influence* (about Japanese lobbyists), Alfred A. Knopf.
Congressional Quarterly, (1979) *The Washington Lobby,* p 129-65.
Emerson, Steven (1985) *The American House of Saud,* Franklin Watts.
Halow, Jos (1989) *Grain: The Political Commodity,* University Press of America.
Hancock, Graham (1989) *Lords of Poverty: the power, prestige and corruption of the international aid business.* Atlantic Monthly Pr. p181.
Heidenheimer, Arnold (1978) *Political Corruption,* Transaction Bks, p 346-57.
Howe and Trott, (1977) *The Power Peddlers,* Doubleday.
Jacoby, Neil H. et al (1977) *Bribery and Extortion in World Business: A Study of Corporate Political Payments Abroad.* MacMillan.
Klitgaard, Robert (1990) *Tropical Gangsters: One Man's Experience with Development and Decadence in Deepest Africa.* HarperCollins BasicBooks.
Linden, Eugene (1976) *The Alms Race: The Impact of Voluntary Aid (CARE) Abroad,* Random Hse.
Moore, R. (1977) *The Washington Connection,* (Korea lobby) Condor
Noonan, J T (1984) *Bribes,* U CA Pr.
Pierce, C. (1986) *How to Solve the Lockheed Case,* Transaction Books.
Rand, C. T. (1975), *Making Democracy Safe for Oil,* Atlantic Mo. Pr.
Schleifer, A. (1993), Corruption, *Q J Econ,* Aug. pp 599-617.
Trento, S B (1992), *The Power House,* St. Martin's Press.

Appendix B
ECONOMIC GROWTH

"When you have eliminated the impossible, whatever remains, *however improbable,* must be the truth." Sherlock Holmes.

———————

The growth of "Special Interests" (corporate influence on legislation) was recognized and resulted in a wave of congressional reform [Witte pp 238-43]. But these reforms were not directed against the rising tide of government spending.

The halt of our economic growth in the 1970s was followed by attempts to explain it. This Appendix ends with a bibliography.

In 1979 [Denison] published *Accounting for Slower Economic Growth*, in which he says "What happened is, to be blunt, a mystery". And then he solved the mystery: in 1985 he published *Trends in American Economic Growth"*. Denison traced the growth stoppage to reduced capital investment, which he traced to Congress's deficit spending. His estimate of the capital shortfall over the 9 years from 1974 to 1982 was $1.47 trillion in 1972 prices [1985, p 8]. Dividing yields $170 billion per year (1972 prices).

Landau (1983) reported that countries with greater government spending grew more slowly. This was confirmed by Carr (1989).

Krugman (1990) linked our stoppage of growth to stoppage of productivity growth. He did not know what is wrong with our productivity, but he later wrote (1994) that neither do the snake-oil-peddling politicians.

Olsen [pp 236, -7] wrote that our growth stoppage was caused by "special interest groups". This book confirms that, and adds quantitative data to support it.

Rauch (1994) agrees that special interests are the problem, and refers to the "parasite economy" (1992).

Chapter 1 of this book found that something was diverting 200 billion

1993 dollars into non-productive channels, starting in the 1970s. This is strictly an empirical observation: middle-class incomes were growing at 3% per year, but stopped in the 1970s. This confirms Denison; in dollars, my data is smaller because inflation has increased consumer prices 50% since his data.

This annual shortfall is cumulative, and adds up to real money. Denison's estimated total gap of $1.47 trillion would be equivalent to $2.2 trillion in 1995 dollars. Worse still, economic growth has never resumed in the 12 years since Denison's data, so there is another 36% of GDP missing, which is $2.3 trillion. Adding these numbers yields $4.5 trillion. If the economy had continued to grow at 3%, this projects to a net worth 42% greater than we now have.

Apologists for congress might say "No Fair! When the congressmen deregulated S&Ls and delayed regulators, they had no idea what a disaster it would cause." My answer to that is, what about Star Wars, the SSC Supercollider -- endless waste of money on abandoned projects.

References:
Carr, Jack L. (1989), Government Size and Economic Growth, *Amer. Econ. Rev.,* v 79 pp 267-71.
Denison, Edward F. (1979) *Accounting for Slower Economic Growth: the United States in the 1970s,* Brookings.
Denison, Edward F. (1985) *Trends in American Economic Growth, 1929 -1982,* Brookings.
Economist (1992), America's Parasite Economy: The Papers that Ate America, Oct. 10, pp 21-4.
Krugman, Paul (1990), *The Age of Diminished Expectations*: U. S. Economic Policy in the 1990s, MIT Press.
Krugman, Paul (1994), *Peddling Prosperity: Economic Sense and Nonsense in the Age of Diminished Expectations*, W. W. Norton.
Landau, Daniel (1982), Government Expenditure and Economic Growth: A Cross-Country (-nation) Study, *Southern Econ Jour,* v49, 783-92.
Olsen, Mancur (1982), *The Rise and Decline of Nations: Economic Growth, Stagflation, and Social Rigidities,* Yale U. Press.
Rauch, Jonathan (1994), *Demosclerosis: The Silent Killer of American Government,* Times Books.
Witte, John F (1985), *The Politics and Development of the Federal*

Income Tax, U. Wisc. Pr.

Bibliography of Economic Growth
Arndt, H. W. (1978) *The Rise and Fall of Economic Growth,* U. Chi. Pr.
Backhaus, Jurgen (1987) *Public Investment and its Effects on the Burden of the Public Debt.* Southern Economics Journal, pp 145 -58 (theory).
Baily, Martin Neil et al (1989) *Brookings Papers on Economic Activity: Microeconomics.* Brookings.
Basalla, George (1988) *The Evolution of Technology,* Cambridge U. Pr.
Bernheim, B. Douglas (1991) *The Vanishing Nest Egg: Reflections on Saving in America.* Priority Press Pubs. (20th Century Fund Paper).
Bosworth, B.P. (1984) *Tax Incentives and Economic Growth,* Brookings.
Bosworth, Barry P. (1993) *Saving and Investment in a Global Economy.* Brookings.
DuBoff, Richard B. (1989) *Accumulation and Power: An Economic History of the United States.* Sharpe.
The Economist (1989) One Hundred Years of Economic Statistics.
The Economist (1994) War of the Worlds, Oct. 1, Inset, pp 1-18.
Fallows, James (1989) *More Like Us: Making America Great Again.* Houghton Mifflin.
Fenwick, Millicent (1982?) *Speaking Up,* Harper & Row.
Flynn, Raymond L. (1991), Agenda for Demestic Recovery: The biggest danger facing America today is .. the pink slip. *Challenge.* Nov/Dec.
Frank, Andre Gunder (1978) *World Accumulation, 1492-1789.* Monthly Review Press.
Freeman, Roger A. (1981) *The Wayward Welfare State,* Hoover Inst. Pr., Stanford, CA.
Frumkin, Norman (1992) *Tracking America's Economy.* Sharpe.
Galbraith, James K. (1989?) *Balancing Acts,*
Gilder, George (1993) Wealth and Poverty Revisited, *The American Spectator,* July pp32 - 37.
Haas, Lawrence J. (1990) *Running on Empty: Bush, Congress and the Politics of a Bankrupt Government.* Business One Irwin.
Halow, Joseph (1989) *U.S. Grain: The Political Commodity,* University Pr. of America. Good history.
Hazlett, Henry (1979) *Economics in One Lesson.* Arlington House.
Hsieh, Ching-yao et al (1978) *A Short Introduction to Modern Growth Theory,* University Press of America.
Johnson, Chalmers et al (1989) *Politics and Productivity: The Real Story of Why Japan Works.* Harper & Row, Ballinger.
Kendrick, John W. (1977) *Understanding Productivity: An Introduction to the Dynamics of Productivity Change.* Johns Hopkins U. Pr.
Kennedy, Paul (1987) *The Rise and Fall of the Great Powers.* Random House, Vintage Books.
Krugman, Paul (1990) *The Age of Diminished Expectations: U. S. Economic Policy in the 1990s.* MIT Press.
Kuehner, Charles D. (1978) *Capital and Job Formation: our nation's 3rd-century challenge,* Dow Jones-Irwin.

Lekachman, Robert (1972) *National Income and the Public Welfare.* Random House.
Leontief, Wassily (1968) Input-Output Analysis, *International Encyclopedia of the Social Sciences,* 7:345 -54.
McKinney, Jerome B. et al (1986) *Fraud, Waste and Abuse in Government: Causes, Consequences and Cures,* ISHI Pubs.
McKinnon, R. I. (1973) *Money & Capital in Economic Development,* Brookings.
Marsden, Keith (1983) Taxes and Growth. *Finance and Development,* Sept. pp 40 -43. Evidence from 20 countries suggests that those with lower taxes experienced more rapid growth.
Marston, David W. (1991) *How Lawyers Use Our Secret Rules to Get Rich, Get Sex, Get Even .. and Get Away With It,* Wm. Morrow.
Modigliani, Franco (1986) Life Cycle, Individual Thrift, and the Wealth of Nations, *Science.* v234, 7 Nov. pp 704 -712.
Mueller, D. (ed) (1983) *The Political Economy of Growth,* Yale U. Pr.
Myrdal, Gunnar (1957) *Rich Lands and Poor: The Road to World Prosperity.* Harper & Bros.
Nye, Joseph S. Jr. (1990) *The Misleading Metaphor of Decline Atlantic Monthly,* March, pp 86 -94.
Olsen, Mancur (1982) *The Rise and Decline of Nations: Economic Growth, Stagflation, and Social Rigidities.* Yale U. Pr.
Osterfeld, David (1992) *Prosperity versus Planning: How Government Stifles Economic Growth.* Oxford U. Pr.
Patterson, J et al (1994) *The Second American Revolution.* Wm. Morrow.
Payne, James E. et al (1993) *Defense Spending and Economic Growth.* Westview.
Rauch, Jonathan (1992?) *America's Parasite Economy* ....
Rimmer, Douglas (1973) *Macromancy: The Ideology of "development economics",* Inst. of Economic Affairs.
Rosen, Sam (1963,1972) *National Income and Other Social Accounts.* Holt, Rinehard & Winston.
Rosenberg, Nathan et al (1990) Science, Technology and the Western Miracle, *Scientific American,* v 263 No 5, November pp 42 -54.
Solow, R. M. (1970) *Growth Theory: An Exposition.* Oxford U. Press.
Steuerle, C. Eugene (1985) *Taxes, Loans, and Inflation: How the Nation's Wealth Becomes Misallocated,* Brookings.
Usher, D (1980) *The Measurement of Economic Growth,* Columbia U. Pr.

Appendix C
THE INEFFICIENCY OF BUREAUCRACIES

Abstract: In a complex process, the overall efficiency can be surprisingly low.   In this context, *complex* does not mean *complicated;* it means many-layered.

Definition: The *efficiency* of each layer in the process would be 100% only if there are no errors, false starts or duplication of effort.

Farming is one example of a process with many layers: (1) planning the layout and timing of the crops, (2) planting, (3) cultivation, (4) harvesting.   Inefficiency in *any* of those processes can affect the cash yield realized for the crop.   Timing is important not only for weather conditions after planting, but also for realizing a good price in a fluctuating market.   Planting with too much or too little fertilizer can reduce the crop.   Inadequate weeding and aeration of the soil can reduce the yield, as can harvesting too early or too late.   An adverse market can reduce the cash yield.

The point here is that in a process with many layers *each* layer can affect the overall efficiency, because they all tend to multiply together. (Efficiencies never multiply *up,* they always multiply *down* because they are 100% or less.)   To take an example, if each of the above four processes is 80% efficient, the overall efficiency can be found by multiplying 0.8 four times: the result is only 0.41, or 41%.   Clearly, successful farming is difficult.

This principle is important, so it will be repeated in different words: (1) the unfavorable weather after planting caused 20% of the seeds to die, (2) fertilizing was uneven, so 20% of the remaining plants died, (3) weeds choked out and killed 20% of the remaining crop plants, and (4) late harvesting caused 20% more of the crop to die.

This principle of multiplying-down is shown by Fig. 1.   The efficiency of each layer (80%) is shown on the horizontal scale.   (Each layer is called a *factor* of production.   There are many layers here, so they are called *multi-factors*).   The middle line represents the four multi-factors listed above.   The overall efficiency that results, 41%, can be interpolated on the vertical scale.

Part of the trouble with government spending is that many of the most influential people in government are appointed because they helped win an election, not because of merit. And they in turn hire their cronies. Fig. 1 shows what often happens: if their productivity is only 50% instead of 80%, four layers of bureacracy produce an overall efficiency of only 6%!

Most government spending is many-layered: for example defense procurement (a) goes through many decision-points even before the purchase is made, (b) goes through many decisions in the allocation of money by congress, and (c) goes through many decisions during its design and fabrication. Figure 1 shows that when more layers are added (the right-hand line represents 8 layers), the output is hopelessly low.

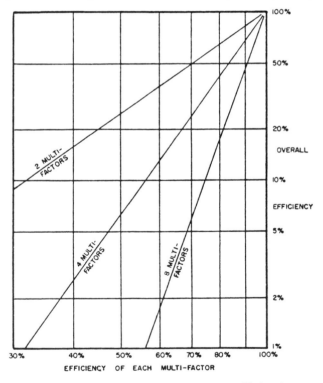

Fig. 1. Result of multiplying-down of individual efficiencies.

Appendix D
THE PAC MULTIPLIER FOR CONGRESS

Abstract
It is desired to estimate the importance of bribery in the economy. A previous paper [Brooks 1995] dealt with the Savings and Loan failures of the 1980s, and reported that the PAC multiplier was unexpectedly high for congress. This paper explores other congressional spending to see whether the S&L cases were typical for Congress.

For other congressional spending the PAC multiplier was indeed very high: about 4,000.

1. Introduction

A bribe is money etc. offered to procure favors[1]. The "bribes" in the title are PAC (Political Action Committee) funds or other campaign contributions.

The approach in this paper is to estimate the PAC multiplier. This ratio is multiplied in Appendix A, by the total bribes [published by Makinson], to estimate the total cost of bribery for Congress.

There is an obstacle here: for most congressional spending there is no reliable estimate of *cost*. Who could be trusted to make an unbiased estimate of the value to society of an aircraft carrier? Consequently, this study is limited to those cases in which the cost is unequivocal.

Two defense contract examples are included in which congressional spending bought nothing. The other cases are concerned with farm price supports.

These farm price supports are a blend of subsidy payments to the producer, and of import duties or other restrictions which increase the price to the public. Direct payments cost the taxpayer directly; import restrictions cost the consumer in higher prices. The price increases have been estimated in the references. Both the subsidy payments and the price increases are dollar costs, and they are both borne by either the taxpayers or the consumers, i.e. the general public.

Import duties on sugar date from 1789 [Sanderson p 24-5]. The growing of sugar and the distilling of rum were well-established in the colonies before the American revolution. The import duties protected this domestic industry, and they had a revenue motive as well. Sources of funds for the new national government were severely restricted by the constitution, but it did permit import duties for the protection of domestic products.

The Great Depression of the 1930s brought hardship and ruin to many small farmers. This was important politically, because at that time 21% of Americans made their living on farms [World Almanac]. So the New Deal broadened price supports to include many other crops, among them tobacco and dairy foods.

But it is now 60 years later and things have changed: (a) the younger generation left the farm for city jobs, (b) machines boosted the productivity of the workers remaining on the farms, and (c) the capital required to buy the machines encouraged the aggregation of small farms into large agribusinesses, for economies of scale. Now only 2.5% make their living from farming [World Almanac], and they are employees. Financially, they are doing well: the full-time farm family has 39% more income than the average family, and a net worth exceeding $800,000 [Bovard pp 48-50].

Price supports benefit the *owner(s)* of farms. "Subsidies take from the poor and give to the rich" [Economist Dec 12, 92 pp S5(4); Sanderson p 29]. "The small farmers ... are helped relatively little ..." [Schultze p 30]. In 60 years of congressional give-aways, the farm owners have learned to evade individual limits by such ruses as fictitiously subdividing their farms. The sugar subsidy gives "a quarter of a million dollars *each*" to 12,000 sugar growers [Stern p 168]. "The USDA runs farm programs with a contempt for taxpayers' money that is often mind-boggling", [Bovard p 259].

Now price supports buy nothing useful to society, but are merely welfare for the rich. This is generally recognized, and every election campaign brings talk of reforms, but they don't happen in the USA. New Zealand leads in abolition of farm price supports: farmers now receive only 4% of their income in subsidies, and they like it that way. They "would move a vote of no confidence in a minister who advocated subsidies for them or anyone else in the economy," (Farm Minister John Falloon [Economist Dec. 12, 92 p S14(3)]).

2. The Data

Table 1 summarizes the data, and details are given in the remainder of this section.

2.1 Sugar

Congress supports the sugar industry with direct payments and import restrictions. The cost to the public is $3 billion[2] per year [Stern p 168].

2.1.1 From 1985 to 1990, the PAC payments totaled $2.6 million [Stern p 169]. The PAC multiplier was then ($15 billion)/($2.6 million) = 5,770.

2.1.2 In 1984 and 85, the PAC payments were $1½ million [Stern p 169, 170]. The PAC multiplier was then ($6 billion)/($1½ million) = 4,000.

2.2 Dairy

PAC funding:

1991,-2: $877,500 [Makinson 1994]
1989,-90: $1.37 million [Makinson 1992]
1987,-8: $1.61 million [Makinson 1990]
1985,-6: $1.61 million (estimated to be the same as above)
1983,84: $3.3 million [Stern pp 171,2]

COST:

2.2.1 1985-90:

Cost of subsidy: 2.77 billion. Price increase: 11.5 billion. Total = $14.27 billion [Stern pp 171,2]. Total bribe: 4.59 million. Cost/bribe = 3,109.

2.2.2 1987:   Cost of subsidy = $1.4 billion. Cost of price increase: $1.2 billion. Total = $2.6 billion [Sanderson p 52]. Bribe: $805,000[3]. Cost/bribe = 3,230.

2.2.3 1972:   Total cost: $500-700 million [Sobel p 17]. Bribe: $722,500 [Sobel p 25]. Cost/bribe = 830.

Table 1.
PAC multiplier for Congress.

Ref.	Year	Total Cost	Bribe[3]	Ratio
		Sugar		
2.1.1	1984-85	\$ 6 billion[2]	\$1.5 million	4,000
2.1.2	1985-90	15 billion	2.6 million	5,770
		Dairy		
2.2.1	1985-90	14.27 billion	4.59 million	3,109
2.2.2	1987	2.6 billion	805 thousand	3,230
2.2.3	1972	600 million	722,500	830
		All Farm Produce		
2.3.1	1991	34.7 billion	12.45 million	2,787
2.3.2	1990	35.28 billion	8.9 million	3,964
2.3.3	1989	32.16 billion	8.9 million[3]	3,613
2.3.4	1988	36.94 billion	6.35 million	5,817
2.3.5	1987	43 billion	6.35 million	6,772
2.3.6	1986	44 billion	5.88 million	7,483
2.3.7	1985	39 billion	5.88 million	6,633
2.3.8	1984	29 billion	5.425 million	5,346
2.3.9	1983	36 billion	5.425 million	6,636
		Tobacco		
2.4	1984	400 million	150 thousand	2,667
		Commodity Traders		
2.5	1983-84	300 million	70,500	4,255
		Defense Contracts		
2.6.1	1986	25 million	6,500	3,846
2.6.2	1982	300 million	5,000	60,000

2.3 Overall farm products

The PAC bribes below are from Makinson[3] [ ]

The outlays below are from OECD Press Release for 1992:

2.3.1 1991: Federal outlays and consumer price increases: $34.7 billion. Cost of bribe: $12.45 million. PAC multiplier = 2,787.

2.3.2 1990: Federal outlays and consumer price increases: $35.28 billion. Cost of bribe: $8.9 million. PAC multiplier = 3,964.

2.3.3 1989: Federal outlays and consumer price increases: $32.16 billion. Cost of bribe: $8.9 million. PAC multiplier = 3,613.

2.3.4 1988: Federal outlays and consumer price increases: $36.94 billion. Cost of bribe: $6.35 million. PAC multiplier = 5,817.

The outlays below are from [Bovard pp 257,-8]:

2.3.5 1987:   Federal outlays: $30 billion. Consumer price increases: $13 billion. Cost of bribe: $6.35 million. PAC multiplier = 6,772.

2.3.6 1986:   Federal outlays: $31 billion. Consumer price increases: $13 billion. Cost of bribe: $5.88 million [Smith]. PAC multiplier = 7,483.

2.3.7 1985:   Federal outlays: $26 billion. Consumer price increases: $13 billion. Bribe: $5.88 million [Smith]. PAC multiplier = 6,633.

2.3.8 1984: Federal outlays: $16 billion. Consumer price increases: $13 billion. Bribe: $5.425 million [Smith].
PAC multiplier = 5,346.

2.3.9 1983: Federal outlays: $23 billion. Consumer price increases: $13 billion. Bribe: $5.425 million [Smith]. PAC multiplier = 6,636.

2.4 Tobacco

The story about tobacco costs is complicated.

First, the direct cost to the public in higher prices is calculated as above: 1984: $400 million [Sanderson p 50]. PAC data for 1984 are not available, so it is extrapolated from 1988 and 1992 data as $150,000 (estimated). This gives a PAC multiplier of 2,667.

But price is not the only cost. Smokers also pay a price in medical bills and shorter life. The added medical costs are now nearly *$50 billion* a year. By one estimate [Rubenstein], smokers may be "paying their own way" by dying earlier. But the medical costs are so large that they out-weigh the product cost in the paragraph ˄bove; any change such as inflation in medical costs would strongly affect the PAC multiplier.

2.5 Commodity Traders

Congress voted down a proposed tax which would yield $300 million [Stern p 182]. Bribe = $70,500 [Stern p 183]. Cost/bribe = 4,255.

2.6 Defense Contracting

2.6.1 1986:   Defense contractor Dravo overran a contract price by $25 million. Instead of renegotiating with the Navy, Dravo convinced Senator Arlen Specter to tack a grant onto the next defense appropriation bill. Dravo had contributed $4,000 to the senator's campaign before the grant, and $2,500 afterward [Stern p 186]. Cost/bribe = ($25 million)/($6,500) = 3,846.

2.6.2 1982:   Chairman Addabbo (deceased) of the House Appropriations subcommittee on defense spending had been a "prime mover" in ending Avco's monopoly on manufacture of engines for the M-1 tank. In 1983 he reversed himself and voted to continue the monopoly, even though a bid from a competing firm would have saved the taxpayers $300 million. The contractor gave Addabbo $5,000 in campaign contributions [Stern p 186,-7, quoting Wall St. Journal, Oct. 13, 1983]. Cost/bribe = 60,000.

3. Discussion of Results

3.1 Was bribery the <u>Sole</u> cause of the cost?

In some cases the bribe may not be the *only* cause for the cost; ideology might play a part also. Two alternative ways to handle this are:
1. Take the PAC multipliers as they are reported above at their face value, or
2. Try to compensate for the partial cause-effect relationship. Stern [pp 176,-7] suggests how to do this. For example, if half the cost is attributed to the bribe, then the PAC multipliers should be reduced to ½ the values reported in Section 2.

There are arguments in favor of either viewpoint; the method being used should be clearly indicated.

3.2 Transfer Efficiency: the Loot/Cost ratio

Congress transferred money from the public to the farm owners. Because the owners motivated these transfers with bribes, they can be called "loot". How efficient was the transfer?

Price guarantees, subsidies and import restrictions pay an overhead cost in reporting and administration. They also distort the market, tending toward price increases, loss of domestic market share and overproduction. This overproduction is especially costly for storing perishable produce like butter and cheese.

This complexity makes the transfer efficiency difficult to calculate. Sanderson [pp 407-9] estimated it at 41%, but wrote that "the true ratios are probably even lower."

Bovard [p 66] wrote that the transfer efficiency was 1/5 in the early 30s, but it has decreased and now is 1/10.

The Economist [6/27/92 p 21(3)] reported that the transfer efficiency is 1/3. This is adopted in this paper as the median estimated transfer efficiency.

Some of the sales are not captured by domestic producers, but appear in competing foreign markets as producer and/or consumer benefits. The remainder is waste, that is, deadweight-loss.

3.3 Return On "Investment": the Loot/Bribe ratio:

Snyder [p 17] discusses "investing" in a congressman. The yield on this investment would be the PAC multiplier found in Section 3.1 multiplied by the Loot/Cost ratio from Section 3.2: 4,127 x 1/3 = 1,376. Investing in farm and defense PACs yielded a terrific return.

3.4 Data Accuracy:

Bribery data are sparse (Table 1 contains only 18 data points), and their values are spread widely. In Table 1 the quartiles are 61% above the median and 22% below it. Therefore the error in the value of the central tendency (median) is expected to be substantial. The number of decimal places is not at all intended to indicate accuracy; they are carried out solely to aid the reader in tracing their derivation if desired.

A crude idea of the error of the median can be obtained by deleting 10% of the high data points and then 10% of the low data points, and noting how these deletions shift the resulting median value. Doing this yields medians of 3,982 and 4,800, a spread of 818, or 20%, justifying the use of one or two decimal places. This is merely a rough gage of the *minimum* error; it is not at all rigorous because it is sensitive to the size of the intervals between the middle data points.

3.5 Generality of Results:

This analysis is based on those few cases where the cost of government spending is known or has been estimated. If interest in the

PAC multiplier should spread, future research can produce more accurate estimates of the cost of government spending, and how it varies with factors such as the nature of Congress's spending, calendar time, etc.

4. Conclusions

The median PAC multiplier was 4,127. The cost was borne by the public in taxes and prices.

This is less than one-third of the ratios reported previously for Congress in the S&L cases [Brooks], but it is still very large.

The transfer efficiency was 1/3. The other 2/3 of the cost was deadweight loss, that is, waste.

The motivation for giving campaign contributions is clear: the Return On Investment was greater than 1,000.

Notes

1   The Concise Oxford Dictionary.
2   One billion is 1,000,000,000.
3   Elections are held on the even-numbered years. The bribes were smoothed-out by averaging the election year with the previous year.

References

Bovard, J. (1991). *The Farm Fiasco,* ICS Press.

Brooks, Herb (1995), The Cost of Bribery and Self-Dealing in the S&L Failures, *Human Systems Management.*

Brusca, R. (1990) Economic Currents, *Financial World,* Dec 11 p81.

Cabot, E. and Sheekey, K. (1990) PACs are Bad News for Democracy, *Across the Board,* v27 p 11(3) December.

Demaris, O. (1974) *Dirty Business: The Corporate-Political Money-Power Game,* Harper & Row.

Drew, E. (1983) *Politics and Money: The New Road to Corruption,* Macmillan.

The Economist (1992) "The Trough: America's Farm Subsidies", June 27 p 21(3).

The Economist (1992) "They Reap as They Sow (Farm Subsidies)", Dec. 12 p S5(4).

Ibid, p S14(3).

Ferguson, A. (June 1985) *The Sugar Price Support Program,* US Cane Sugar Refiners Assoc.

Green, M. with Waldman, M. (1982) *Who Runs Congress?* Dell.

Johnson, D. G. et al (1985) *Agricultural Policy and Trade,* NYU Pr. p.162.

Loeb, L. (1975) *American Politics,* Macmillan.

Makinson, L. (1990 -92 -94), *Open Secrets,* Congressional Quarterly.

OECD (Office for Economic Co-operation and Development) (1992), *Agricultural Policies, Markets and Trade: Monitoring the Outlook,* Press Release 14 May, SG/Press(92)39, Paris.

Rubenstein, Ed. (1994) Ifs, ands and Butts, *National Review,* v46, August 15 p16.

Sabato, L. (1984) *PAC Power,* W. W. Norton.

Sanderson, F., ed. (1990). *Agricultural Protectionism in the Industrialized World,* Resources for the Future.

Schultze, C. (1971). *The Distribution of Farm Subsidies: Who Gets the Benefits?* Brookings Instn.

Smith, P. (1989) PACs: Farmers' $8-million Muscle Man, *Successful Farming,* April.

Snyder, J. (1992) Long-Term Investing in Politicians; or Give Early, Give Often, *Journal of Law and Economics,* v 35, April.

Sobel, L., ed. (1977). *Corruption in Business* Facts on File.

Stern, Philip M. (1992). *Still The Best Congress Money Can Buy,* Regnery Gateway.

Thomas, B. (1994) *Club Fed: Power, Money, Sex and Violence on Capitol Hill,* Charles Scribner's Sons.

Wall Street Journal, (1983) October 13.

Welch, W. (1982), Campaign Contributions and Legislative Voting: Milk Money and Dairy Price Supports, *The Western Political Quarterly,* v 35 No 4 December 1982.

Wessel, J. (1983). *Trading the Future: Farm Exports and the Concentration of Economic Power in Our Food Economy,* Institute for Food and Development Policy.

The World Almanac and Book of Facts, (1993) p 122.

Appendix E
THE GOVERNMENT'S GDP REPORTS ARE BIASED IN ITS FAVOR

".. most of what our government appears to do is make-believe for the benefit of those in office." Charles Peters.

Abstract

The government's reports show that in 1991 it spent 42% of the U. S. GDP (Gross Domestic Product). However, that report is biased. The government *understates* its spending. The true fraction spent by government is estimated to be 53 to 62%; the government lets us spend only 38 to 47% of what we earn.

As the fraction of GDP spent by government continues to expand, the bias in its reports increases along with it.

The bias occurs because of the way the government calculates the GDP: it adds its own spending to private spending. This method is faulty. Appendix D found excessive waste in government spending. It buys very little *Real Product*, yet this method of calculation gives government spending equal weight with private spending in estimating the total Product. "Government does not create wealth ..", it simply shifts it about [Payne   ]. To measure total product by the *amount spent* is faulty.

Can this bias be removed? What is the true fraction of our GDP spent by government? This paper attempts to estimate it. At first glance, it would seem that the problem could be solved by estimating the Productivity of government spending. The trouble is that such an estimate would depend on the ideology of the estimators. If it were done by government, it would still be biased. It is too important for that.

In any case, reliable data do not exist, so this paper assumes bracketing values for the Productivity of government spending. Based on these assumed values, the estimated overstatement of GDP is 25 to 50%. History is plotted for this adjusted GD*Real*P (*Real* Product) and for the increasing fraction of GD*Real*P spent by government.

1. Summary

The strength and growth of the nation's economy are measured [19,30,38,43,47,55] in terms of the Gross Domestic Product (GDP). "Domestic" means produced within the 50 states.

The GDP numbers are calculated by the U. S. Census Bureau. The government calculates the GDP in a strange way: *all government spending is counted as "Product"* [54]. The United Nations use a similar method.

There are widespread reports of waste in government spending, some of which are cited in section 3.1 below. The literature is virtually one-sided in this; there are many advocates of government spending, and Garment [24] wrote that political scandals may or may not improve government. But there are few reports that government is productive or efficient, and those words are not in the index of Garment's book.

Von Hoffman [62] reported waste in private industry also, but industry is subject to the profit motive and to competition. There are no such controls on government.

This study begins here. The premise of this paper is that government spending is less productive economically than private buying on the competitive market. Their ratio is here called P, defined in section 3.2 below.

It is desirable to calculate the GDP in a less biased and more meaningful way, by including only the *real Product* purchased by government spending. For the purposes of this paper, this less-biased GDP is called the Gross Domestic *Real* Product (GD*Real*P).

In this Appendix, the term "*Real* Product" does **not** mean "adjusted to compensate for inflation". It means "if the excessive waste could be squeezed out".

To calculate the GD**Real**P directly would require knowledge of the real product purchased by government spending, or a number for P, neither of which is available. Instead, this paper attacks the problem the other way around: the relative productivity of government spending (P) is made a parameter of the graphs. The reader can assume a value for P and then find in the graphs the GD**Real**P, and the fraction of GD**Real**P spent by government.

Figure 1 shows the multiplying factor for converting GDP to GD*Real*P, and Figure 2 shows the fraction of *Real* Product spent by government. Figures 3 and 4 show the *histories* of the GD*Real*P and of the fraction of Real Product spent by government.

If enough interest should develop in the productivity of government spending (P), its estimated value might be a suitable topic for research.

2. Components Used by Government in Calculating the GDP

The Gross Domestic Product numbers are presently calculated and reported by the Bureau of the Census. The Total GDP as reported includes all government spending, Federal, State and Local [54].

In Table 1 the left-hand column shows the components of the GDP calculation currently in use by the Census Bureau, adapted from [54]. The sources for the numbers are cited in section 6 below. The right-hand column shows whether the spending in that component is classified as productive or non-productive for the purposes of this paper.

TYPE OF SPENDING	PRODUCTIVE OR NON-PRODUCTIVE
Personal consumption of Goods and Services:	Productive
Private investment:	Productive
Government purchases of goods & services:	Partly productive (P), partly non-productive (1-P)

Table 1. Components of the reported GDP (left-hand column) and whether the component is productive or non-productive (right-hand column).

3. The Gross Domestic *Real* Product (GD*Real*P)

It is desired to estimate the fraction of GDP that is *productive*, so that the non-productive fraction of government spending can be subtracted from the GDP total.

What fraction of government spending is productive? Friedman wrote [23] ".. why (is)[1] .. a government enterprise so much less efficient than a comparable private enterprise." His answer was that self-interest is served by different actions in the private sphere than in the public sphere. George Will wrote [64] "(Government)[1] officials .. make neither shoes, nor butter nor poetry. They make rules." Peters wrote [49] "The first key to understanding Washington is 'make-believe.'" O'Rourke wrote [46] "Giving money and power to government is like giving whiskey and car keys to teen-age boys."

3.1 Waste in Government Spending [41]: This paper classifies spending waste under several headings:

3.1.1 Spending that is Partly Productive: Examples: roads, schools, housing; but Ray Archer reported [5] that road-building legislation is full of pork. Some roads and streets are being re-worked most of the time. Martino [40] described science pork.

With regard to the schools, a recent study [34,37] found that nearly half of U. S. adults are barely literate. Much of the problem with our schools rests with the bureaucracy: Munro [44] reported that in the New York secondary school district, the fraction of funds reaching the classroom is only 32% -- the bureaucracies "soak up the rest of the money".

Allen [2] and Welfeld [63] wrote that the mismanagement of HUD (Department of Housing and Urban Development) was a scandal. Bowsher [10] described government financial mismanagement in general, DioGuardi [17] reported Congressional irresponsibility from the point of view of an insider and a CPA, and Atkinson [6] wrote that the State is exploitive and incompetent.

---

[1]*(Text in parentheses added).*

3.1.2 Projects Not Needed: Political "pork". Many recent examples are given in each of these references: [8] Birnbaum, [25] Grace, [26] Gross, [35] Kelly, [39] Marimow, [50] Podolsky, [52] Reisner.

3.1.3 Give-aways Resulting from Political Mismanagement: Examples: politicians are giving away our technology, Tolchin [56]; a large fraction of foreign aid is wasted, Hancock [28]; the financial collapse and bail-out of New York City was unnecessary, DioGuardi [17], Rogow [53].

3.1.4 Not Economically Productive: Examples: paying the farm industry to *not* grow crops, Bovard [9a]; man/woman in Space.

3.1.5 Abandoned Projects: Examples: the nuclear rocket motor, the campaign in North Korea, the Vietnam War, the DIVADS gun, the advanced solid fuel rocket motor, FADA (the Federal Asset Disposition Association [16]), the wool and mohair subsidy, and the superconducting super collider.

3.1.6 Unreported Government Costs to Society: There are some social costs that government causes but does not report as such, for example: (a) "off-budget" spending [7], (b) the "parasite economy" [18], (c) waste and excessive profit in monopolies sheltered from competition by government, (d) waste caused by inflation [22], (e) lost productivity and reduced capital investment for tax avoidance, Payne [48], (f) costs to businesses of collecting taxes for the government [48], and (g) fees paid by the public for accountants, consultants, and lawyers to comply with tax rules which are unnecessarily complex.

*3.1.7 Some government spending is actually **de**structive.* Public health is reportedly damaged by tobacco use, so George Will wrote [65] that the tobacco growers' subsidies are destructive.

3.1.8 One very important incentive for government spending is *bribery.* Bribery causes wasteful spending (Appendix).

3.2 Productivity of Government Spending

For the purposes of this paper, P is defined as the Economic Productivity of government spending relative to private spending:

P = (Economic Productivity of government spending)/(Economic Productivity of private spending)

"Economic Productivity" is here defined by what it is *not*: It is not the kind of wasteful spending listed in section 3.1 above.

These values -- P, and the Economic Productivity of government spending -- are not known. The readers of this paper may have an opinion about the relative efficiency of government spending, but it would be asking too much for all readers to agree on a number. Most of us including the writer, have idealogical or political bias. Therefore, P was made a parameter of the graphs. The reader can adopt his/her own preference for P according to individual information and beliefs, and can interpolate between the curves if desired. Some readers might prefer P=0.5 for the productivity of government spending; this implies that they think its productivity is half the productivity of private industry. Other readers will think P is nearer 0.2. The writer counts himself in this group; however it is not the purpose of this paper to defend that opinion.

For those who think the productivity of government spending is *higher* than 0.5, Brooks [11] showed that productivity tends to suffer where the levels of management are many, as in government including the legislature, and its contractors. The individual efficiencies multiply together. As an example, if management is otherwise perfect, it takes only 5 management levels at 70% efficiency to drag the overall efficienty down to 17% (0.7^5). Appendix C explains in more detail.

3.3 The Correction Factors

It is desired to estimate a new value for the GD*Real*P, adjusted for the non-productivity of some government spending. To find the GDRealP, the non-productive government spending:

(1-P) x (Total government spending)

was subtracted from the (nominal) GDP as reported by the Census Bureau.

Figure 1 shows the resulting conversion factor (multiplier) for finding the GD*Real*P when given the government's figures. The straight lines in Figure 1 denote various assumptions for the productivity (P) of government spending.

Figure 1 shows that for government productivity P less than 1, the Census Bureau overstates the GDP. For example, in 1991 the reported GDP was $5.67 trillion, and the reported government spending was $2.38 trillion, or 42% of that total. If the reader assumes that the productivity of government spending (P) is 0.5, from Figure 1 it can be found that the GD*Real*P was 79% of the reported GDP, or $4.49 trillion. In this case, the GDP value reported by the Census Bureau was exaggerated (overstated) by (5.67/4.49)-1, or 26%. If on the other hand, the reader assumes P=0.2, then Figure 1 shows a conversion factor of about 67%, leading to $3.77 trillion for GD*Real*P. In this case the GDP overstatement was (5.67/3.77)-1, or 50%.

Overstating the reported GDP has another effect as well: it *understates* the fraction of GD*Real*P spent by government. If the reader again assumes P=0.5, then figure 2 shows that when the government spent a *reported* 42% of the GDP (as it did in 1991) it spent *53%* of GDRealP. The fraction of GD*Real*P spent by government was 26% greater than it reported.

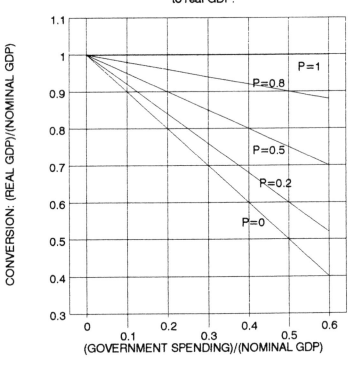

Fig. 1. Conversion factor from nominal
to real GDP.

Fig. 2, showing fraction of real GDP
spent by gov't (vertical scale).

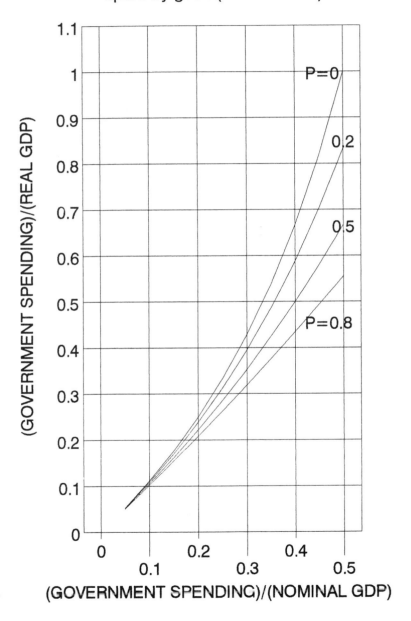

(GOVERNMENT SPENDING)/(REAL GDP)

P=0

0.2

0.5

P=0.8

(GOVERNMENT SPENDING)/(NOMINAL GDP)

If on the other hand the reader assumes P=0.2, then Figure 2 shows that the fraction spent by government was *62%* of GDRealP, and the fraction of GD*Real*P spent by government was 50% greater than it reported.

Because GDP is in the denominator, the P=0.2 and P=0 curves rise rapidly at the right-hand edge of Figure 2.

4. The History of GDP and Government Spending

Figure 3 shows the history of the GDP per capita, in 1987 dollars. The top curve, labeled P=1, shows the history for GDP as reported by the government's Census Bureau, and the lower curves show the history of the *Real* Product, adjusted for assumed values for productivity P of 0.5, 0.2 and 0 respectively.

Figure 4 shows the fraction of GDP spent since 1900 by all levels of government, Federal, State and Local. The curve labeled P=1 shows the values reported by the Census Bureau. The other three curves show the fraction spent by government adjusted for various assumed values of its productivity. These adjusted curves were calculated by dividing government spending by the GDRealP calculated in section 3.3 above.

In the graphs, the effects of an intermediate assumption for P can be obtained by interpolating between the curves.

4.1 Discussion

The American Revolution of 1776-81 was a tax revolt [1], and it was successful for more than a century: In 1902, only 7.7% of GDP was spent by all levels of government (Figure 4). Of that 7.7%, the Federal government spent 2.25%, or 29% of all government spending.

Figure 3 shows the adverse effect of the Depression on real incomes (1932, -33), and Figure 4 shows that government spending rose in the failed Keynesian attempt at "pump priming" (as it was then known). The spending increase turned out to be permanent.

Since 1902, the U.S.A. has participated in six major wars and at least four minor wars; and each war boosted government spending. One of the plots in Figure 4 shows that government spending exceeded the GDP in World War II (the early 1940's); this indicates deficit spending; during the war, the government sold war bonds aggressively and successfully.

During that War (1942) the Federal government began requiring employers to withhold income tax. This was for "the duration", to pay for the war, but after the shooting war came the "cold war", and tax withholding became permanent. The Federal government is now the biggest spender. In 1991 Federal government spending was 56% of the total for all governments.

The fraction of GDRealP spent by government is unknown, because the relative Economic Productivity (P) of government spending is unknown. If government spending is between 20 and 50% productive (relatively), then the government spends between 62 and 53% of GDRealP (Figures 2 and 4). We all work for the government now.

What fraction of GDP *should* the government spend? Calleo [14] wrote "how and why has the deficit grown to ... a mechanism for national decline". Kennedy [36]: "... in Relative Decline." Eventually, deficit spending turns into taxes (to pay interest on the debt) and "... high taxes retard growth" [Gilder, 24a]. Hazlitt [31]: "the larger the percentage of national income taken by taxes the greater the deterrent to private production and employment." For the average U. S. citizen, personal savings and investment are low: B. Friedman [21], Pollin [51]. Real GDP growth averaged only 1% since 1966 (figure 3, 0.5>P>0.2).

Now federal spending promises to become even greater. A major item of spending is health care, which now costs 14% of the *nominal* GDP (total of public and private costs). Because the nominal GDP is overstated (section 3.3 above), this translates to a larger fraction of the GDRealP: 17.5% if P=0.5, or 20.6% if P=0.2. And now the Federal government is planning to further expand its spending to supply health care to everyone; and health care has its own problems [27,29].

5. Conclusions.

5.1 Because the nonproductive fraction of government spending is counted-in, government reports of Gross Domestic *Real* Product have been exaggerated (overstated). Since 1966, the growth in *real* Product averaged only about 1% per year.

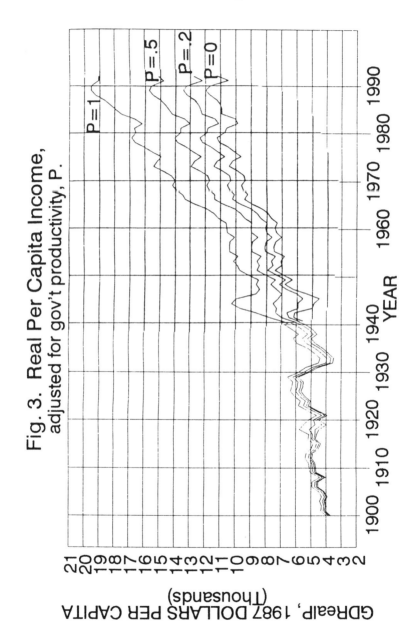

Fig. 3. Real Per Capita Income, adjusted for gov't productivity, P.

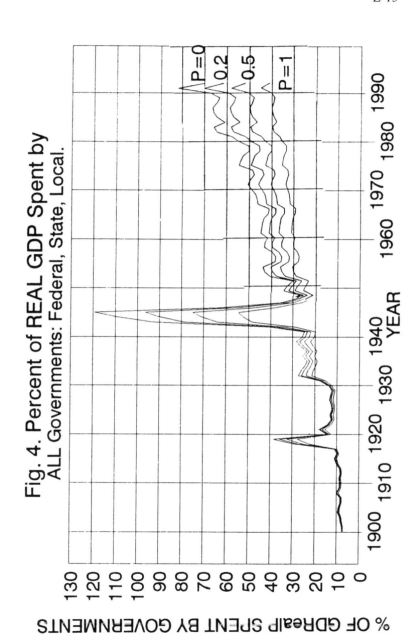

Fig. 4. Percent of REAL GDP Spent by
ALL Governments: Federal, State, Local.

5.2 Because reported GDP is overstated, the fraction of *Real* Product (GD*Real*P) being spent by government has been understated.

5.3 To remove the bias,
a. The GDP needs to be calculated in a different way, so that it includes the value of Real Product only; or,
b. The economic productivity (P) of government spending needs to be estimated.

6. Data Sources

The graphs are based on (a) yearly data for the real GDP per capita, "real" meaning adjusted for inflation, that is, for the cost of living, and (b) yearly data on the total nominal spending for all levels of government (Federal, State and Local) divided by the nominal GDP. Reference [58] was used for data through 1970, and reference [57] for more recent data. Exception: until about 1984, references [57,58] reported GNP data but not GDP. GDP data were therefore obtained from [59] back through 1960. Before 1960, GDP data could not be located, and GNP data were used instead. The difference would be almost imperceptible in the graphs: In 1960 the GDP differed from GNP by only 2%, and it was even less before 1960. Offshore and over-the-border production (for tax advantage) became important economically only after 1960, and especially after the 1970's price shocks on foreign oil.

References

[1] Adams, Charles, *For Good and Evil: the Impact of Taxes on the Course of Civilization,* Madison Books, 1993.

[2] Allen, Steve, *Ripoff: The Corruption that Plagues America,* Lyle Stuart, 1979 p 22.

[3] Andreski, Stanslav, Kleptocracy as a System of Government in Africa, Chapt. 35 of [32] p 346,-57.

[4] Archer, Ray, From Potato Research to Carp Control, What Your New Taxes Will Buy, *Ariz. Republic,* (edit.), Aug. 23, 1993.

[5] Archer, Ray, 'Inside the Imperial Congress' [20], Why the Nation's Business is Undone, *Az. Republic,* (edit.), May 10, 1993.

[6] Atkinson, Rodney, *Government Against the People: The Economics of Political Exploitation,* Camelot Press, (Southampton) 1986, p 140.

[7] Bennett, James T. and DiLorenzo, Thomas J., *Underground Government: The Off-Budget Public Sector,* Cato Inst., 1983.

[8] Birnbaum, Jeffrey H., *The Lobbyists: How Influence Peddlers Get Their Way in Washington,* Times Books, 1992 p 16,80,292-6.

[9] Boulton, David, *The Grease Machine,* Harper & Row, 1978.

[9a] Bovard, James, *The Farm Fiasco: How federal agriculture policy squanders billions of dollars a year. sacrifices the poor to the rich, and gives congressmen and bureaucrats vast arbitrary power over American citizens,* ICS Press, 1990.

[10] Bowsher, Charles A., *Financial Management Issues,* Transition Series, U.S.Govt Printing Office GAO/OCG-93-4TR, Dec. 1992.

[11] Brooks, Herb, Efficiency of Complex Projects, *IEEE Trans. on Engineering. Mgmt.,* v. EM-13 No. 3, Sept. 1966.

[12] Brooks, Herb, The Cost of Bribery, *Human Systems Management,* 12 (1993) 215-210, IOS Press, Amsterdam.

[13] Brooks, Robert C., Apologies for Political Corruption, Chapt. 51 of [32], p 501,-9.

[14] Calleo, David P., *The Bankrupting of America: How the Federal Budget is Impoverishing the Nation,* Morrow, 1992 p 23,-4.

[15] Congressional Quarterly, *The Washington Lobby,* 3d ed, 1979, p 129-165.

[16] Day, Kathleen, S&L Hell: *The People and Politics Behind the $1*

Trillion Savings and Loan Scandal, W. W. Norton, 1993.

[17] DioGuardi, Joseph J., CPA, *Unaccountable Congress: It Doesn't Add Up,* Regnery Gateway, 1992.

[18] *The Economist* editorial staff, America's Parasite Economy, Oct. 10, 1992, pp 21-24.

[19] *The Economist* editorial staff, Running to Stand Still, Nov. 10, 1990, pg. 19-22.

[19a] Emerson, Steven, *The American House of Saud: the Secret Petrodollar Connection,* Franklin Watts, 1985.

[20] Felton, Eric, *The Ruling Class: Inside the Imperial Congress,* (abridged ed.), Heritage Foundation, 1993.

[20] Friedman, Benjamin, *Day of Reckoning: The Consequences of American Economic Policy,* Random House Vintage, 1989 p 7,11.

[22] Friedman, Milton, *Money Mischief: Episodes in Monetary History,* HBJ, 1992 p191, 208-10, 221.

[23] Friedman, Milton, *Why Government Is the Problem,* Essays in Public Policy, Hoover Inst., Stanford Univ., 1993, p. 8.

[24] Garment, Suzanne, *Scandal: the Culture of Mistrust in American Politics,* Times, Random House, 1991 p 302, -4.

[24a] Gilder, George, Wealth and Poverty Revisited, *American Spectator,* July 1993 p32-37.

[25] Grace, J. Peter, *Burning Money: the Waste of Your Tax Dollars,* Macmillan, 1984.

[26] Gross, Martin L., *The Government Racket: Washington Waste from A to Z,* Bantam Books, July 1992.

[27] Halvorson, George C., *Strong Medicine,* Random House, 1993.

[28] Hancock, Graham, *Lords of Poverty: the Power, Prestige, and Corruption of the International Aid Business,* Atlantic Monthly Pr., 1989 p 181.

[29] Harmer, Ruth Mulvey, *American Medical Avarice,* Abelard-Schuman, 1975.

[30] Harvard Business Review Panel, How Real is America's Decline, HBR, Sep-Oct 1992, pp 162-174.

[31] Hazlitt, Henry, *Economics in One Lesson, Arlington House, 1979 p 39.*

[32] Heidenheimer, Arnold J., ed., *Political Corruption: Readings in Comparative Analysis,* Transaction Books, 1978.

[33] Howe, Russell Warren and Trott, Sarah Hayes, *The Power Peddlers: How Lobbyists Mold America's Foreign Policy,* Doubleday, 1977.

[34] Jordan, Mary, Nearly Half of U. S. Adults are Barely Literate, *Az. Republic,* Sep. 9, 1993, pg. A1. Also see [37].

[35] Kelly, Brian, *Adventures in Porkland: How Washington Wastes Your Money and Why They Won't Stop,* Villard Books, 1992.

[36] Kennedy, Paul, *The Rise and Fall of the Great Powers: Economic Change and Military Conflict from 1500 to 2000,* Random House, 1987, p 514.

[37] Kirsch, Irwin S., *Adult Literacy in America,* U. S. Congress. Also see [34].

[38] Kurtzman, Joel, *The Decline and Crash of the American Economy,* W. W. Norton, 1988.

[39] Marimow, William K., Capitol Till (a review of [26,35]), *New York Times Book Review,* October 25, 1992, pp 8,9.

[40] Martino, Joseph Paul, *Science Funding: Politics and Porkbarrel,* Transaction Pubs., 1992.

[41] McKinney, Jerome B., and Johnston, Michael, *Fraud, Waste and Abuse in Government: Causes, Consequences and Cures,* ISHI publications (Phila.), 1986.

[42] Miller, Nathan, *Stealing from America: a History of Corruption from Jamestown to Reagan,* Paragon House, Aug. 1992.

[43] Mueller, Dennis C., ed., *The Political Economy of Growth,* Yale U. Pr., 1983.

[44] Munro, Douglas P., Study of Classroom Expenditures, Heritage Foundation, 1993.

[45] Myrdal, Gunnar, Corruption: Its Causes and Effects, Chapt. 55 of [32], p 540,-5, especially p 541.

[46] O'Rourke, P. J., *Parliament of Whores: a Lone Humorist Attempts to Explain the Entire U. S. Government,* Atlantic Monthly Press, 1991, rear cover of book.

[47] Osterfeld, David, *Prosperity versus Planning:* How Government Stifles Economic Growth, Oxford U. Pr., 1992.

[48] Payne, James L., *Costly Returns: The Burdens of the U.S. Tax System,* ICS Press, 1993, p150.

[49] Peters, Charles, How Washington Really Works, *Washington Monthly,* Jan/Feb 1993, pp 43+.

[50] Podolsky, J. D. and Sugden, Jane, Mr. Fussbudget (a review of [26]), *People magazine,* 8/9/93.

[51] Pollin, Robert, Exchange, *The Nation,* p 586.

[52] Reisner, Marc, *Cadillac Desert: The American West and its Disappearing Water,* Penguin, 1987.

[53] Rogow, Arnold A. and Lasswell, J. D., The City Boss: Game Politician or Gain Politician, *Political Corruption: Readings in Comparative Analysis,* Arnold J. Heidenheimer, ed., Transaction Books, 1970.

[54] Samuelson, Paul A., and Nordhaus, William D., *Economics,* 14th ed., McGraw-Hill, 1992.

[55] Shiau, Alan, *Competitiveness Index 1993,* Council on Competitiveness, 900 17th St. NW, Ste 1050, Washington, DC 20006. Also see [60].

[56] Tolchin, Martin and Susan, *Selling Our Security: The Erosion of America's Assets,* Alfred A. Knopf, 1992.

[57] U. S. Bureau of the Census, *Statistical Abstract of the United States,* various issues through 1992.

[58] U. S. Bureau of the Census, *Historical Statistics of the United States: Colonial Times to 1970, parts 1 & 2,* 1975.

[59] U. S. Bureau of Economic Analysis, *Business Statistics, 1963-91,* June, 1992.

[60] *U. S. News and World Report,* November 2, 1992, pg. 11.

[61] van Klaveren, Jacob, Corruption: The Special Case of the United States, Chapt 26 of [32], p 269-275.

[62] von Hoffman, Nicholas, *Capitalist Fools: Tales of American Business from Carnegie to Forbes to the Milken Gang,* Doubleday, 1992.

[63] Welfeld, Irving, *HUD Scandals: Howling Headlines and Silent Fiascos,* Transaction Press, 1992.

[64] Will, George, So, the Culprits Are Now the Cure?, *Newsweek,* Sept. 20, 1993, p.68.

[65] Will, George, Tobacco War is Picking Up, *Ariz. Republic,* Feb. 7, 1991.

Bibliography:
Wolff, Edward N. (1987) *Growth, Accumulation and Unproductive Activity,* Cambridge U. Pr.

Index